Kieler Studien

Institut für Weltwirtschaft an der Universität Kiel

Herausgegeben von Herbert Giersch

217

Frank D. Weiss et al.

Trade Policy
in West Germany

Authors:
Bernhard Heitger,
Karl Heinz Jüttemeier (†), Grant Kirkpatrick,
Gernot Klepper, Frank D. Weiss,

J.C.B. MOHR (PAUL SIEBECK) TÜBINGEN

ISSN 0340-6989

Kieler Studien

Institut für Weltwirtschaft an der Universität Kiel

Herausgegeben von Herbert Giersch

217

Frank D. Weiss et al.

Trade Policy in West Germany

Authors:
Bernhard Heitger,
Karl Heinz Jüttemeier (†), Grant Kirkpatrick,
Gernot Klepper, Frank D. Weiss,

J.C.B. MOHR (PAUL SIEBECK) TÜBINGEN

ISSN 0340-6989

CIP-Titelaufnahme der Deutschen Bibliothek

Trade policy in West Germany / Frank D. Weiss ... - Tübingen
: Mohr, 1988
    (Kieler Studien ; 217)
    ISBN 3-16-345427-5 brosch.
    ISBN 3-16-345428-3 Gewebe
NE: Weiss, Frank D. [Mitverf.] ; GT

        Distributed by
        Westview Press, Inc.
        5500 Central Avenue
        Boulder, Colorado 80301

Schriftleitung: Hubertus Müller-Groeling

Institut für Weltwirtschaft an der Universität Kiel
J. C. B. Mohr (Paul Siebeck) Tübingen 1988
Alle Rechte vorbehalten
Ohne ausdrückliche Genehmigung des Verlages ist es auch nicht
gestattet, den Band oder Teile daraus
auf photomechanischem Wege (Photokopie, Mikrokopie) zu vervielfältigen
Printed in Germany
ISSN 0340-6989

ISBN 0-8133-0901-8 (Westview)

This book is dedicated to the
memory of our colleague

Karl Heinz Jüttemeier

Contents

List of Tables

List of Figures

Abbreviations and Acronyms

AHC	Allied High Commission
AVI	Arbeitsgemeinschaft der Eisenverarbeitenden Industrie
BDA	Bundesvereinigung der Deutschen Arbeitgeberver-bände
BDI	Bundesverband der Deutschen Industrie
BdI	Bund der Industriellen
BICO	Bipartite Control Office
CAP	Common Agricultural Policy
CDI	Centralverband Deutscher Industrieller
CDU	Christian Democratic Union
CPE	Centrally-Planned Economy
CRESH	Constant Ratio Elasticity of Substitution Homothetic
CSU	Christian Social Union
DGB	Deutscher Gewerkschaftsbund
DHT	Deutscher Handelstag
DIHT	Deutscher Industrie- und Handelstag
EC	European Community
ECEFP	Executive Committee on Economic Foreign Policy
ECSC	European Coal and Steel Community
ERP	European Recovery Program
FDP	Free Democratic Party
GATT	General Agreement on Tariffs and Trade
GDP	Gross Domestic Product
GDR	German Democratic Republic
GNP	Gross National Product
IPCOG	Informal Policy Committee on Germany
JCS	Joint Chiefs of Staff
JEIA	Joint Export-Import Agency
LDC	Less Developed Country
LTA	Long-Term Agreement Regarding International Trade in Cotton Textiles
MFA	Multifiber Arrangement
MFN	Most Favored Nation
NATO	North Atlantic Treaty Organization
NIC	Newly Industrializing Country
NTB	Nontariff Barrier
OECD	Organization for Economic Cooperation and Development
OMGUS	Office of Military Government United States
RCA	Revealed Comparative Advantage
R&D	Research and Development
RDI	Reichsverband der Deutschen Industrie
RM	Reichsmark
SPD	Social Democratic Party
STA	Short-Term Arrangement Regarding International Trade in Cotton Textiles
UN	United Nations
VDMA	Verein Deutscher Maschinenbau Anstalten
VER	Voluntary Export Restraint

Preface

This study on trade policy in West Germany is part of the Kiel Institute's research program analyzing the longer-run pattern of structural change. The Uruguay Round of multilateral trade negotiations, as well as a resurgence of interest in trade policy as a form of industrial policy, enhances the topicality of the subject. The study presents a systematic quantification of the effects of protection policy in West Germany.

This policy promotes very few industries, of course at the expense of all other activities. Subsidies and quotas under the control of the national government are the main instruments. Trade policy is shown to be particularly protective where special pressure groups have emerged that are not subject to the discipline of the comprehensive interest representation so characteristic of West Germany. Protective policy is generally directed at industries suffering from competition of cheaper foreign sources of supply. It is often explicitly designed to slow down the exit of redundant firms; it appears to go hand in hand with depressed rates of labor productivity growth, particularly in small firms. Under these conditions, external liberalization would certainly enhance welfare; it would do so even more, and would effectively promote employment, if it went along with an internal liberalization, particularly of the labor market.

The project was directed by Frank D. Weiss, who carried out the work on tariffs, effective assistance and on political economy, and who also prepared the final draft. The substantive work on subsidies was undertaken by the late Karl Heinz Jüttemeier. Gernot Klepper carried out the research on the history of German trade policy; Bernhard Heitger and Frank D. Weiss analyzed the consequences of trade policy; and Grant Kirkpatrick, who maintained the Institute's general equilibrium model, is responsible for the liberalization simulations. At the start of the project, Doris Witteler equally contributed to this study.

The authors would like to express their gratitude to Juergen B. Donges for his continual encouragement and for his critical comments on the penultimate draft. In addition, they acknowledge stimulating discussions with many colleagues at the Kiel Institute. Bernhard Klein and Fiona Short deserve gratitude for their meticulous editorial guidance, and Helga Huß and Petra Walter for the efficient and cheerful typing of the manuscript.

The core of the research work was financed by a grant from the Alfried Krupp von Bohlen und Halbach Stiftung, whose generosity the Kiel Institute gratefully acknowledges.

Kiel, August 1988   Herbert Giersch

Die Gedanken sind zollfrei.
Aber man hat doch Scherereien.

Karl Kraus

I. Introduction

1. The period between the onset of the Tokyo Round multilateral tariff reductions and the Uruguay Round has been turbulent for the international economy and for international economic policymaking. Sharp swings in industrial countries' terms of trade, the steady emergence of a new group of countries exporting industrial products and following in the footsteps of Japan and the appearance of apparently persistent differences in current external accounts of many countries, accompanied by successive waves of disinflation policy, all contributed to a widespread malaise from which relief was often sought, and sometimes granted, in the form of protection from foreign suppliers. For a time, in the mid-1970's, it looked as if the world economy would slide once more, as during the Great Contraction, into substantial increases in foreign trade protection, and so intensify and prolong the structural and adjustment pressures from which most established industrial countries were suffering. Appropriately, the period has been called "the era of the new protectionism". It witnessed a broadening of restrictions in the international textile and clothing trade, the imposition of substantial restrictions in the steel industry, and eventually international skirmishes fought with pasta and veal, automobiles and machine tools. Subsidies increased in many countries, and a bewildering array of often temporary trade barriers was imposed selectively on individual products and countries.

2. The era poses a paradox, however. International trade did not break down, as during the 1930's. The European Community (EC) expanded from six to ten, and then to twelve member states. The European Community signed a free-trade agreement on industrial products with the European Free Trade Area (EFTA). The Tokyo Round of multilateral

tariff reductions did succeed in bringing down nominal tariffs. More recently, the United States signed a bilateral free-trade treaty with Canada. The Uruguay Round of multilateral trade barrier reductions got underway with a broadened agenda compared to previous rounds, and with at least a promise to desist from further practices inconsistent with GATT principles.

3. Under these conditions it is important to gain an understanding of what the trade policy of a country widely considered to have liberal trading interests has been, how that policy has come about, and, in view of the ongoing Uruguay Round, how it is likely to evolve in the near future. The first important step in this direction is systematic quantification of trade policy measures actually applied. While much evidence - quantitative and anecdotal - about trade policy in West Germany exists, not enough of it is systematic, so that it is difficult to confront hypotheses about the causes and consequences of trade policy with the relevant facts.

4. From outside Europe, it might appear that studying trade policy in one country, when that country is a member of the EC, is a pointless task. Appearance deceives. Trade policy, except tariff policy, even in fields of activity which formally fall under Community auspices, is overwhelmingly a matter of national prerogative. But tariff policy has become quantitatively less important over time and is subject to yet wider international agreement. In agriculture, one of two industries formally controlled from Brussels, national price levels differ significantly among countries, and roughly half of subsidies to agriculture are paid for by the national government in West Germany's case. In the coal and steel complex, the first economic activity to come under international auspices in the present EC, essentially a system of rules has been established which permit national governments to carry out their own policy in such a way as to minimize consequent costs for other member states. Similarly, national governments set import quotas under the multifiber agreement (MFA) themselves. The EC merely acts as formal intermediary between member states and nonmember states. Finally, each community member can invoke Article 115 of the Treaty of Rome and exclude the good in question from common treatment altogether. There is doubtless

tension between Community institutions and national governments for control over various aspects of policy. When the chips are down, national governments win.

5. The trade and trade policy problems of the last decade and a half have gone hand in hand with a resurgence of interest in the theory of trade policy. Two parallel sets of research interests and results have emerged, one concerned with the causes of trade policy measures, the other concerned with the consequences of such measures. The political economy approach to trade policy seeks to find the causes of trade policy in interest group formation and interaction with government. Trade policy is attributed to rent-seeking behavior on the part of interest groups and rent-granting behavior on the part of government. West Germany is a particularly well furnished laboratory for examining the relevance of these ideas, because an influential, almost institutionalized set of distinctive interest groups is in place. The industrial policy approach to trade, on the other hand, seeks effects of trade and industrial policy measures in the presence of economies of scale, and hence, non perfectly competitive markets. Here, too, West Germany is an appropriate laboratory for evaluating these ideas because many different kinds of policy measures are in place and have been changed differentially across industries over the last decade and a half.

6. Particularly since the era of the new protectionism ended and the uneasy trade policy truce emerged, interest in the costs of protection has waved and interest in the potential benefits of protection (under strictly circumscribed conditions to be sure) has waxed. One reason for the switch in emphasis might be the paucity of harder quantitative evidence on the extent of protective measures. Applied studies of whole economies typically estimated the costs of protection attributable to the one instrument - the tariff - whose relative and absolute importance had declined to near insignificance. Typical estimates of the costs of protection have been on the order of one half to one percent of GNP. Such orders of magnitude will understandably reduce excitement about the cost of distortions engendered by trade policy. Consideration of subsidies and other nontariff barriers (NTB's) alters such conclusions.

4

7. Equally importantly, other significant institutional conditions have usually been ignored. In macroeconomics, recognition has been growing, though of course there is no unanimity, that there may be something particular about labor market conditions in Europe. This special feature has often been subsumed under "labor market rigidity" or "real wage rigidity". While this study does not address the issue directly, the consequences of such institutions for the effect of trade liberalization can be simulated. This is done with a general equilibrium model of the West German economy. It turns out that the flexibility of the real wage is crucial in determining the outcome of trade liberalization. Such a policy would be for more effective if coupled with an internal liberalization.

8. The next chapter quantitatively maps out what trade policies are in fact undertaken on an industry-by-industry basis. The evidence is systematized by implementing Corden's [1966] concept of effective protection. The estimates include the effects of tariffs, subsidies, and the important NTB's. Then the causes of those policies are examined. Chapter III seeks to relate various categories of subsidies to policy intentions and policy institutions. Chapter IV adopts a political economy framework for explaining total assistance to industry in Germany. Institutions which seem to worsen policy outcomes are identified. Some of the elements which are recognized as driving trade policy, such as foreign policy considerations and ideology, are difficult to examine on an interindustry basis. Therefore, Chapter V adopts a historical perspective on German tariffs to show that these two forces were very important in determining policy outcomes. Afterwards the consequences of present day trade policies are subjected to scrutiny. Chapter VI focuses on the role of trade policy in codetermining the interindustry pattern of specialization, or competitiveness, and seeks systematic relationships between changes in interindustry protection and some of the apparent objects of policy. Then, in Chapter VII the effects of trade liberalization on employment and income are simulated under alternative labor market institutions. Finally, the study ends with a brief summary of results, a discussion of possible further research, and some conclusions for shaping policy.

II. Effective Assistance to Industries in West Germany - A Quantification for the Mid-1970's and Mid-1980's

9. Soon after the successful completion of the Kennedy Round of multi-lateral tariff costs, the world economy was hit by the great supply shock of the first oil price hike in 1973. One general response to the ensuing structural dislocation and aggregate contraction consisted of increased protection from foreign competition for some affected industries or individual activities. This occurred both in the United States and in the EC, including West Germany. For a time, it seemed as though a general surge in protection was either already underway, or was at least imminent. Thus, the period of the 1970's has been called the "era of the new protectionism". Yet, it was during this period that the Tokyo Round of trade negotiations got under way and was completed. Nominal tariffs at least on industrial products were reduced. The period as a whole, right up until the present, reveals the imposition of a bewildering array of specific and general trade policy measures, some temporary, some at least semipermanent. It is therefore difficult to characterize the period descriptively in a systematic way, much less to map out the consequences of policy for trade and welfare, or investigate the causes of trade policy, or to gain an informed opinion about the prospects for the ongoing Uruguay Round of trade barrier reductions. As a prelude to such analysis, trade and industrial policy for the period must be systematically quantified. While individual sectors have been studied for various countries or regions, this task has not been undertaken for any of the larger industrial countries as a whole.

1. Measurement Concepts

10. The purpose of this chapter, then, is to quantify trade policy measures for the recent past in a systematic way. To this end, Corden's [1966] concept of effective protection is implemented for two points in time - one about the mid-1970's, or before the onset of the Tokyo

Round, and one about the mid-1980's, when the last of the agreed tariff cuts was completed. The reason for using Corden's almost quarter-century-old concept is that it is the simplest general equilibrium formulation of protection, and so is parsimonious with respect to information requirements. Put slightly differently, the data collection effort can be targeted to obtain good characterizations of nominal protection (1) and preserve a certain amount of interindustry detail. In addition, these results can be compared with the results of past periods and other countries obtained by other investigators. Not least, the concept is fairly straightforward.

11. The point of the effective rate concept is to capture the effect of protection of output on the size of an economic activity when inputs used in the production of that output are also protected (2). Put differently, actual value added of an activity is compared to value added if there were no tariffs, quantitative restrictions, or subsidies. In algebraic terms:

$$[1] \quad ERP_j = \frac{1 - \sum_{i=1}^{n} a_{ij}}{\frac{1}{1+t_j} - \sum_{i=1}^{n} \frac{a_{ij}}{1+t_i}} - 1$$

where a_{ij} is the material input/output coefficient, i.e. the share of input i in output j at domestic prices and t_j is the nominal ad valorem tariff rate or its equivalent.

The numerator measures value added at domestic prices, and the denominator measures value added at world prices. There, gross output is deflated by the output tariff, and the input shares are deflated by the corresponding input tariffs. The measures are exact under the assumptions that foreign output is in perfectly elastic supply (relative prices are fixed) and that the elasticity of substitution among material inputs is zero.

(1) Chapter VII takes the opposite route - a general equilibrium formulation without the strict confines of the effective rate concept is applied, but at the cost of some interindustry detail.
(2) See the exposition in Corden [1971, pp. 35-44].

12. The concept can be adapted to express the change in net value added attributable to the protective system, rather than the gross value added [Hiemenz, Rabenau, 1973]. This means taking account of the effect of the tariff structure on the value of depreciation of capital goods. Then [1] becomes:

$$[2] \quad ERP_j = \frac{1 - \sum_{i=1}^{n} a_{ij} - \sum_{i=1}^{n} A_{ij}}{\frac{1}{1+t_j} - \sum_{i=1}^{n} \frac{a_{ij}}{1+t_i} - \sum_{i=1}^{n} \frac{A_{ij}}{1+t_i}} - 1$$

where A_{ij} is the share of depreciation of the i-th capital good in gross value added of sector j. In practice, total depreciation in each sector is deflated by an unweighted average tariff for six investment goods.

13. Not all production is sold behind tariff walls; some is exported and sold at world market prices. Assuming that the share of value added in gross output that is exported is identical to the share of value added in gross output that is sold behind tariff walls makes the required adjustment to the formula for the effective rate of assistance straightforward. The share of gross output (unity), instead of being deflated by $1+t_j$, is deflated by $1+t_j$ adjusted for the share of gross output sold behind tariff walls d_j, so that [2] becomes:

$$[3] \quad ERP_j = \frac{1 - \sum_{i=1}^{n} a_{ij}}{\frac{1}{1+d_j t_j} - \sum_{i=1}^{n} \frac{a_{ij}}{1+t_i}} - 1.$$

Here, d_j, the share of output sold behind tariff walls, is not the share of production sold domestically only, but rather the share of production sold in the EC. For tariffs this argument is straightforward, because all EC countries share the same tariff schedule.

14. Since a major aim of this study is to include the effects of NTB's in the quantification, and since it is widely appreciated that individual EC

member countries can apply for national treatment of certain goods according to Article 115 of the Treaty of Rome, the question of how to treat German exports of such goods to the EC countries imposing separate national treatment arises immediately, and must be settled in principle at the outset. There is good reason to believe that the nominal rate of protection of the corresponding goods in the countries applying national treatment rises only to the level of the least protective member state (1). The reason is easy to see: free intercommunity trade in substitute goods drives down nominal protection to the lowest level imposed by any one community country. But by all accounts, West Germany is the country that exempts goods from community treatment least, as Table 1 shows. Hence, nominal protection in the other community countries would tend to be driven down to the German level. In summary, the effective protection calculations can be undertaken using German nominal rates, explicit and implicit.

Table 1 - National Treatment by EC Countries According to Article 115, 1973-1985

	1973	1975	1977	1979	1981	1983	1985
	cases, EC total						
MFA goods(a)	8	12	37	176	89	123	81
Agriculture	6	10	2	3	2	5	5
Other	20	14	22	58	25	31	39
Total	34	36	61	237	116	159	125
	percent distribution						
Benelux	25.0	16.7	27.0	19.9	16.9	12.2	3.2
Denmark	0.0	0.0	0.0	1.1	0.0	0.0	-
France	62.5	42.7	32.4	42.6	39.3	29.3	44.0
West Germany	0.0	0.0	21.6	3.4	1.1	3.3	-
Ireland	0.0	0.0	2.7	14.2	27.0	38.2	24.0
Italy	12.5	33.3	2.7	3.4	6.7	6.5	16.8
United Kingdom	0.0	8.3	13.5	15.3	9.0	10.6	12.0
Total	100.0	100.0	100.0	100.0	100.0	100.0	100.0
(a) Multifiber Arrangement goods.							

Source: Dicke et al. [1987].

_____

(1) This argument has been advanced by Hamilton [1986].

15. Production subsidies are easy to integrate into this framework. Given fixed output and input prices, a production subsidy increases gross output of the industry receiving the subsidy proportionately. Hence, the numerator of [1] changes; value added at domestic prices becomes:

$$[4] \quad ERA_j = \frac{1 + s_j - \sum\limits_{i=1}^{n} a_{ij}}{\dfrac{1}{1 + d_j t_j} - \sum\limits_{i=1}^{n} \dfrac{a_{ij}}{1 + t_i}} - 1$$

where s_j is the subsidy per unit of gross output in industry j [Corden, 1971, p. 42]. This s_j, the rate of subsidy of gross output, is measured at distorted domestic prices, and has been called the "producer subsidy equivalent" [OECD, 1987]. In analogy to the rate of nominal tariff protection, it may also be called the "nominal rate of subsidization". The combined effective protect of tariffs and subsidies, called an Effective Rate of Assistance, can be expressed as the sum of the effective rate of tariff protection and an effective rate of subsidization:

$$[5] \quad ERA_j = ERP_j + \frac{s_j}{\dfrac{1}{1 + d_j t_j} - \sum\limits_{i=1}^{n} \dfrac{a_{ij}}{1 + t_i}}$$

Multiplying the numerator and denominator of the last term by gross output leads to the convenient formulation:

[6] $ERA_j = ERP_j + $ (Subsidy j/Value added at world prices j)

which is equivalent to:

[7] $ERA_j = ERP_j + $ (Subsidy j/(Value added at domestic
    prices j/ERP_j))

and will be used to tabulate the results.

The fixed coefficients formulation ensures that subsidies on gross output will not affect prices, but only quantities. The input-output coefficients themselves are not affected. In economic terms, the recipient of the subsidy increases his gross output by the full amount of the subsidy (free entry), but the value added created in that process is distorted by tariffs, just as the initial value added has been. It must be deflated by the effective rate of tariff protection.

16. In the presence of nontraded goods tracing out the incidence on value added of tariffs and subsidies is complicated slightly, even under a fixed-coefficient technology.

Two extreme simplifying assumptions have been made. Either one can assume with Balassa [1971] that nontraded goods are supplied perfectly elastically, or one can assume with Corden [1971] that they are supplied perfectly inelastically. If they are supplied perfectly elastically, industries of nontraded goods merely pass on their increased costs attributable to tariffs on inputs. Therefore, their effective protection is zero. If nontraded goods are supplied perfectly inelastically, the size of value added in these industries will be affected by tariffs on their inputs and tariffs on traded outputs using them as inputs. Thus, nontraded inputs used intensively in the production of a traded input which is protected by a high nominal tariff will expand; the nontraded input is protected as well. To capture this effect, Corden [1971] lumps nontraded goods with value added.

17. The formula actually used to carry out the calculations is:

$$[8] \quad ERA_j = \frac{1 - \sum\limits_{i=1}^{z} a_{ij}}{\dfrac{1}{1+d_j t_j} - \sum\limits_{i=1}^{n} \dfrac{a_{ij}}{1+t_i} - \sum\limits_{i=n+1}^{z} a_{ij}[\,(w_i + \sum\limits_{k=1}^{n} \dfrac{a_{ki}}{1+t_k}) + \sum\limits_{k=n+1}^{z} a_{ki}(w_k + \sum\limits_{m=1}^{z} \dfrac{a_{mk}}{1+t_m})\,]} - 1$$

The variables t_j, d_j, and a_{ij} have been described above. In the Balassa formula nontraded goods are treated just like traded goods with a zero tariff rate on them. Thus, the summation index $i = 1,...,z$ runs over all goods. In the Corden formula, traded and nontraded goods are treated differently. The summation index $i = 1,...,n$ runs across the traded goods; the index $i = n + 1,...,z$ runs across the nontraded goods. The value added components of nontraded goods are designated w_i, and are subtracted from gross output. The summation index k runs over traded inputs into nontraded inputs, and m is the second round: i.e. nontraded inputs into traded inputs, which go into nontraded inputs. This formula was taken from Donges et al. [1973], but the impact of differential indirect taxes was dropped. In the present study, this is shown as subsidies. Further discussion of the derivation of the two formulas may be found in Balassa [1971, Appendix 1].

2. Quantitative Restrictions and their Implicit Tariffs

18. At first glance, the task of quantifying trade restrictions adopted in West Germany or the EC since the mid-1970's appears unmanageable. A bewildering array of border measures have been adopted, modified, and even dropped with extraordinary frequency. Nevertheless, it has turned out that the attempt to do so has revealed systematic properties of protection policy which have made the task meaningful and relatively straightforward. The initial idea was to collect a catalog of all border measures operative in the EC which affect West Germany and calculate nominal tariff equivalents for each of them. The measures would have to be distinguished by type - mere quotas which lead to an observed discrepancy between domestic and import price, and voluntary export restraints and price undertakings which lead to no such discrepancy, or at least not one observable at the border.

19. The first step in systematizing protection afforded by border NTB's was to collect - on a tariff-line-by-tariff-line basis - all measures operative in West Germany in 1982, be it through the EC, or through national prerogative. They have been classified into quantity restrictions

(quotas and voluntary export restraints - VER's) and price limitations (antidumping duties and price undertakings) and are shown in Table 2. The NTB's found were not weighted by imports for the well understood reason that particularly restrictive barriers receive little weight under such a scheme. A glance at the table reveals how concentrated by industry the measures are.

If one leaves out unilateral German measures still in effect which are aimed against imports from the Centrally-Planned Economies (CPE's), and bears in mind that the restrictions in the ceramics industry, restricting imports from Japan, has been lifted, one is left with a remarkably short list of industries affected:

- coal mining;

- iron and steel; and

- textiles and clothing.

Coal mining, and textiles and clothing have long been exempted from uniform trade treatment, and steel began to be exempted (again) in the mid-1970's. Since 1981 the EC has negotiated bilateral voluntary export restraints (VER's) in steel covering 75-80 percent of EC imports in 1984 [Anjaria et al., 1985]. It is well known that agriculture and food processing are exempt from normal trading rules, and that domestic prices are kept above world market prices by policy intervention (1). Thus, agriculture and food processing have to be added to the list of industries highly protected by nontariff measures.

20. This selection of industries does not at first glance correspond well with other widely-publicized measures to restrict international trade. Thus, in 1981 a bilateral VER was negotiated limiting Japanese automobile exports to the German market to 110 percent of the 1980 level [Bronckers, 1983]. In addition, since 1983 voluntary restraints on Japanese exports to the EC have been negotiated for seven additional product groups (video cassette recorders, color television sets, cathode ray

---

(1) See, e.g. Rodemer [1980] for a presentation of the mechanism and consequences of EC agricultural policy.

Table 2 - Nontariff Barriers in West Germany, 1982 (Percent of Affected
Tariff Lines)

I-O sector	Industry	Quotas and VER's(a)	Antidumping duties and price undertakings
	Mining and manufacturing (total)	11.7	2.5
6	coal mining	45.5	1.7
	Manufacturing intermediate goods		
12	rubber goods	4.6	–
13	stone goods	2.7	–
16	iron and steel	13.8	43.0
17	nonferrous metals	3.0	–
18	foundries	2.9	–
19	drawing mills, cold rolling mills	–	1.6
30	wood	3.3	–
	investment goods		
21	mechanical engineering	1.0	0.1
25	aircraft, aerospace	2.3	–
26	electrical engineering	0.9	1.3
27	precision mechanics, optics, watches	0.4	2.3
	consumer goods		
11	plastic products	–	3.0
14	precision ceramics(b)	28.0	–
15	glass and glass products	9.1	–
29	musical instruments, toys, sporting goods, jewellery	0.6	–
31	wood products(c)	20.5	5.1
35 part	leather, leather goods, shoes	5.9	5.9
35 part	shoes(c)	39.4	–
36	textiles	65.0	–
37	clothing	56.5	–

(a) Voluntary Export Restraints.- (b) Mostly against Japan, since lifted. - (c) Mostly against CPE's.

Source: BMF [1982]; Commission [various issues]; Zeitschrift für Zölle und Verbrauchssteuern [various issues].

tubes, numerically-controlled machine tools, radio receiving and transmission equipment, and quartz watches [Anjaria et al., 1985].

21. But meanwhile, these VER's have been lifted [Financial Times, 1985]. At the same time, the EC has unilaterally raised the tariff rate on video cassette recorders from 8 percent to 14 percent, effective from January 1, 1986. In fact, new registrations of Japanese cars in West

Germany in 1986 amounted to about 25 percent of the market. Aside from the automobile case for a short period of time, only the VER on video cassette recorders seems to have been particularly effective from the outset [Hindley, 1986]. Japanese exports of video cassette recorders to the EC dropped from 5 million units in 1982 to about 1.8 million units in 1985, less than the 2.3 million allowed.

22. Ignoring the temporary restrictions, some of which were or became redundant, and ignoring those industries where very few tariff lines were affected by border measures, generating or collecting estimates of the implicit nominal protection (implicit tariff due to quota or price measure plus explicit tariff) was fairly straightforward. In most cases published or unpublished estimates could be drawn upon, which were extrapolated to the observation years using German import price developments for goods from EC countries and from third countries, when those protective devices actually used lead to a difference of border prices. This applies to agriculture, food processing, and coal. The steel industry and textiles and clothing are generally protected by VER's on third countries. Here, ad hoc procedures were used. For the steel industry, a trade association estimate of the price difference between domestic and third country export markets was available; it was extrapolated with prices published officially. The clothing estimates for the mid-1980's were taken directly from Hamilton [1986], who calculated nominal clothing protection for a host of countries based on his estimates of the rent accruing to Hong Kong producers on account of the Multifiber Arrangement. Roningen and Yeats' [1976] estimate of EC protection in clothing was used for the early period. Textile protection was estimated with unit values of German imports from EG countries, which were compared to unit values of imports from major LDC textile suppliers. It was assumed that the MFN was as restrictive in textiles as in clothing. The ratio of unit value was therefore multiplied by the clothing estimates of the MFA NTB. The results of these collections, calculations and consolidations are shown in Table 3.

23. The movement of some of the implicit nominal protection rates may occasion surprise. It should be noted that agricultural protection varies from year to year to preserve a target level of prices at home in the

Table 3 - Estimates of ad valorem Tariff-Equivalent of Border Trade Barriers (including Tariff) in West Germany (percent)

I-O Sector	Industry	Source values (year)	Extrapolated values 1978	1985
1,2	Agriculture	54.0 (1980-1982)	66.0	50.0
38, 39	Food and Beverages	26.7 (1972)	27.3	20.3
6	Coal Mining	see Text, para. 22.	27.0	47.4
16	Iron and Steel	20.0 (1982)	17.0	25.0
36	Textiles	see Text, para. 22	28.9	26.4
37	Clothing	32.0 (1980-1984)	35.0	32.0

Source: Calculated from Anderson, Tyers [1986], Dicke [1977]; Hamilton [1986]; Roningen, Yeats [1976]; Bundesministerium für Ernährung, Landwirtschaft und Forsten [various issues]; Statistisches Bundesamt [j].

face of the vagaries of the world market. More surprising might be the slight decline observable in clothing protection. But this is consistent with the evolution of world demand [Witteler, 1986a; Hamilton, 1986]. Since the MFA quotas are defined in physical units, their protective effect will be lower when demand is low. The implied slight liberalization of MFA III compared to MFA II was intended; it was recognized that demand growth was low [Cline, 1987, p. 154].

Deardorff and Stern [1985] have criticized the use of what they call "price measures" of the effect of NTB's, namely estimated nominal tariff equivalents, at the conceptual level. They claim that such equivalents do not adequately capture the effect of quota induced trading-up in quality, and emphasize particularly that the effects of quotas on the elasticity of demand for imports is not captured at all. All this is perfectly true, but applies equally to tariffs once one leaves a world of perfectly homogeneous commodities. Deardorff and Stern perhaps ask too much of the data.

The nominal tariff equivalents used here are probably nearer the true values for NTB's in these sectors than the alternative value of zero.

24. The results of this tabulation of nominal protection in industries assisted by substantial NTB's are striking and useful in two respects, no matter how crude the estimates may be. Firstly, the numbers are large

by the standards of tariffs in industrial countries. This means that even committing substantial estimation errors leads to more precise description and analysis than omitting the effects of NTB's altogether. Secondly, in contrast to (almost) all tariffs in the industrial countries, movement of protection is in both directions.

3. Nominal Tariffs

25. The pattern of nominal tariffs in industrial countries has been extensively studied and the changes in the level and pattern of those tariffs implemented during the Tokyo Round are also well understood [see, e.g., Deardorff, Stern, 1984]. A major goal of the Tokyo Round was to reduce the variability of tariff rates, that is to lower high rates proportionately more than low rates. In contrast, the goal of the prior Kennedy Round had been a proportional reduction in tariff rates. The so-called "Swiss formula" was to be used to achieve the reduction of tariff rates and their variance:

$$t_1 = \frac{at_0}{a + t_0}$$

where t_0 and t_1 are the pre and post-Tokyo Round tariff rates respectively and "a" is an arbitrary fixed number. It was set at 16 (percent) for the EC. However, this formula was not strictly adhered to. Exceptions to the rule were permitted if countries compensated their trade partners with further tariff reductions in other sectors.

26. Because of the exceptions to the rule complete enumeration of average tariff levels by industry are required for the pre and post-Tokyo Round periods; simple extrapolation will not do. Such estimates, covering almost all of German industry and almost completely compatible with the German input-output classification of industry have been produced by

Werner, Willms [1984] (1). For present purposes they need to be reaggregated slightly and supplemented; the results are shown in Table 4 and confirm that nominal tariff protection has come down through the Tokyo Round, though there do appear to be some systematic biases in the reduction. Goods of interest to developing countries LDC's experienced lower duty reductions than other goods [see, e.g., Werner, Willms, 1984]. In addition, the well-known phenomenon of tariff escalation may have been exacerbated during the Tokyo Round, particularly in areas where the developing countries are exporters [see, e.g., Balassa, Michelopoulos, 1985; Werner, Willms, 1984]. This seems to be the case in some consumer electronics and footwear fields, though not in cotton textiles, where tariffs are not the important form of protection.

27. Less widely appreciated is another peculiarity of the EC tariff structure, the - selectively used - tariff exemption. The tariff exemption is a zero duty for specific users of the import. In the EC tariff code this is widely applied in the aircraft industry. The tariff code lists by name large commercial airliners, the producers of which need pay no tariff on many inputs they use. In the effective rate calculations, the tariff rate on inputs going into aircraft production will be set at zero, even though this does not capture the situation completely adequately. It is not the aircraft production process as a whole which benefits from the zero duties inputs, but rather only a specific process - namely the final assembly of large commercial aircraft. Now, large commercial airlines are not assembled in West Germany so that the rate of effective tariff protection measured here is probably too high. But the Airbus is assembled in France, subject to the same tariff code. Interestingly, the Airbus engines have been American imports. These make up about 30 percent of the value of the airplane. Thus, the effective tariff protection of Airbus assembly would appear to be quite high. A similar case is the zero duty rate on microchips used in macroframe computers. Here, too, a merely apparent liberality of the tariff code serves to increase the effective protection of a selected production process further upstream. This will

---

(1) That study eschews a strict input-output formulation of effective tariff protection. By giving up some exactness in the definition of value added, it gains slightly more interindustry detail.

18

Table 4 - MFN (a) Nominal Tariff Protection, 1978 and 1985 (percent) (b)

I-O sector	Manufacturing industry	1978	1985
	Intermediate goods		
9	chemicals	10.7	6.5
10	petroleum refining	3.4	2.8
12	rubber goods	9.6	6.3
13	stone goods	5.6	4.2
16	iron and steel	6.5	4.7
17	nonferrous metals	6.4	5.3
18	foundries	7.5	5.2
19	drawing mills, cold rolling mills	7.4	5.2
30	wood	6.7	5.1
32	pulp, paper, paperboard	8.0	5.9
	Investment goods		
20	structural engineering, rolling stock	5.5	4.1
21	mechanical engineering	6.2	4.1
22	electronic data processing equipment	8.1	5.9
23	road vehicles	11.0	10.0
24	shipbuilding	2.8	2.4
25	aircraft, aerospace	8.0	6.5
26	electrical engineering	8.4	5.5
27	precision mechanics, optics, watches	9.4	5.6
28	metal products	7.8	5.6
	Consumer goods		
11	plastic products	11.7	6.1
14	precision ceramics	7.2	5.1
15	glass and glass products	8.5	5.9
29	musical instruments, toys, sporting goods, jewellery	8.3	7.2
31	wood products	9.0	5.4
33	paper and paperboard products	12.2	8.9
34	printing	4.2	2.7
35	leather, leather goods, shoes	7.7	6.1
36	textiles	13.0	9.7
37	clothing	16.1	12.5
	Average	8.8	6.3
	Coefficient of variation	0.355	0.365

(a) Most Favored Nation. - (b) Figures have been slightly reaggreagted compared to source.

Source: Werner, Willms [1984], supplemented by BMF Deutscher Gebrauchszolltariff [1982].

be captured in the effective rate calculations by setting the tariff on deliveries of the electronic data processing industry to itself at the rate of zero.

4. Subsidies and Effective Rates of Assistance

28. Two problems - one of principle and one of practice - stand in the way of integrating subsidization into the effective protection framework. The issue of identifying the subsidy base is the problem of principle. Subsidies are granted on various bases: gross output, material inputs, or primary inputs. These will affect the size of value added in each industry in different ways. For example, a subsidy on gross output will increase domestic value added by the share of value added in gross output (at distorted domestic prices). A subsidy on intermediate input use would, in a general formulation, lead to more intense use of the subsidized input through the substitution effect, and to greater value added in the intermediate goods producing industries, as well as to some increase in value added in the subsidized industry, through the dissipation of the subsidy in producing more output. A direct subsidy of any of the primary factors will shift primary factor proportions towards the subsidized factor, and increase value added indirectly through substitution away from intermediate inputs and directly through subsidy dissipation. If one takes the Leontief fixed coefficient technology seriously, however, substitution effects are absent, and all subsidies are passed on in the form gross output increases. Hence, it is legitimate, though restrictive, to attribute subsidies to gross output, and work out the effective rates on that basis (1).

29. As a practical problem, the definition of subsidies in the national accounts is incomplete. While a category "subsidies to business" is distinguished, for present purposes net current transfers, and gross transfers to business on capital account need to be added. In addition, the subs-

(1) This strong assumption is given up in the smooth technology general equilibrium formulation in Chapter VII.

idy equivalent of the change in receivables, i.e. the difference between market and preferential interest rate loans to the business sector is clearly a subsidy. Moreover, transfer payments to persons, if the recipients are sufficiently restricted in spending their receipts, would have the same effect as direct subsidization of gross output. Differential discriminatory direct tax rates also have the same effect as direct subsidies if they are conditional on income being earned in specific industries. Differences in indirect tax rates could have been accommodated in the effective protection framework: differential indirect tax rates lead to price differences for using sectors and hence influence the effective rate of protection. In the calculations to be undertaken here, they were allocated to subsidies. As a practical matter this is important mainly for the agriculture/food processing complex because a preferential rate of indirect taxation applies there. The tax break on agriculture was allocated to food processing. The rest of the economy is a hardly affected because of the small deliveries of this complex to other industries.

30. No institution in West Germany, public or private, systematically collects the requisite data. The national accounts, while showing transfers to the business sector on capital account, do not show tax revenue foregone through concessionary tax rates, which vary among industries and firms. Biannual official government reports [Deutscher Bundestag, a] do include tax relief, and list about 300 different federal programs, but these are generally incomplete in scope and suffer from periodic changes in the definition of subsidies (1), apparently based on intention, rather than on effect.

31. To overcome these problems, the budgets of all subsidy-granting institutions, including the Federal Government, the eleven state (Länder) governments, a sample of municipalities, the para-fiscal institutions, and the state-owned banks - encompassing the government sector in the national accounts - were compiled. (Government-owned operating enterrises belong to the business sector.) From the budget documents and ancillary sources of information, particularly from government ministries, the government expenditure side of the national accounts was reconstructed in

_____
(1) For a critique, see OECD [1983, pp. 120 ff.].

such a way that every item classed as a subsidy could be allocated to an industry. The items included are (official) subsidies to businesses, net current transfers to businesses, selected transfers to persons, gross transfers to businesses on capital account (1), and the subsidy equivalent of the change in receivables. Tax exemptions were taken from the official subsidy reports, supplemented by some own estimates, and added to the above items to obtain total subsidies (2).

32. The inventory showed that German subsidization policy encompasses roughly 10 000 different budgetary items, which added up to DM120 billion in 1984, far more than is documented by the official subsidy reports of the Federal Government. Table 5 shows subsidy totals for various measuring concepts. The totals shown here include subsidies to housing. The bulk of these subsidies consist of transfer payments to households, which are tied to spending on rent. Hence, they increase the size of the housing sector unambiguously. Nevertheless, the effect of the protective system on the housing sector will not be further analyzed. The reason is not so much because a greater sized housing sector is a result of an obvious social policy - even social policies can and do induce inefficiency if the policy is not carried out in optimal form. Rather, in spite of housing subsidies alone inducing an unambiguous expansion in the housing sector, modelling their gross effect goes beyond the scope of this study: Germany had nation-wide rent control from 1973 to 1985. The beginning of that period saw inflation rates that most likely swamped any change in equilibrium relative prices. Hence, this sector is ignored, except in one or two descriptive tables in the chapter on the coherence of subsidization policy. The producer subsidy equivalent (Corden's "s") for the economy as a whole, measured at distorted domestic prices, rises somewhat according to two of the measurement concepts used - the national accounts, and the one adopted in this study. Official reports tend to understate the rise in subsidies, because of omissions and because of the neglect of subsidy equivalents of state guaranteed loans. The ratio of subsidies to value added is reported here as a description device to fix

---

(1) Transfers from businesses to government on capital account are small, and are nondiscriminatory, being mostly payments for property development in lieu of taxes.
(2) For a more detailed description of the procedure adopted, see Jüttemeier [1984].

22

Table 5 - Subsidies (a) in West Germany According to Different Measurement Concepts, 1973-1984

Source	1973	1974	1980	1981	1984
National accounts (b)					
billion DM	27.4	29.3	49.3	48.2	62.3
producer subsidy equivalent (c) (percent)	1.3	1.3	1.4	1.3	1.5
subsidy/value added (d) (percent)	4.2	4.2	4.8	4.5	5.0
Subsidy reports of the Federal Government (e)					
billion DM	41.7	44.1	65.3	65.5	74.5
producer subsidy equivalent (c) (percent)	2.0	1.9	1.9	1.8	1.8
subsidy/value added (d) (percent)	6.4	6.3	6.3	6.1	6.0
Kiel Institute (e)					
billion DM	45.9	62.5	102.7	103.0	120.0
producer subsidy equivalent (c) (percent)	2.2	2.7	2.9	2.8	2.9
subsidy/value added (d) (percent)	7.0	9.0	9.9	9.6	9.7
subsidies per person engaged (DM)	2430	2720	4610	4670	5890

(a) Business sector, housing and private nonprofit institutions. - (b) Subsidies plus capital transfers. - (c) Subsidies/gross output at domestic prices. - (d) At domestic prices. - (e) Financial assistance plus tax exemptions.

Source: Calculated from Deutscher Bundestag [a]; Statistisches Bundesamt [h]; see also the government budgets in bibliography and para. 31

orders of magnitude. It has no normative significance beyond the statement that if there were no border measures restricting trade, the figures given would correspond to effective protection according to both the Balassa and Corden methods. The interindustry distribution of subsidies is shown in Table 6 for 1974 and 1984. The table sheds some light on subsidization policy. With the exception of a handful of industries, manufacturing activities are hardly subsidized at all, and the average rate of subsidization has scarcely increased. Subsidization policy is rather directed to agriculture, mining, transportation and selected non-traded goods.

Table 6 - Interindustry Pattern of Nominal Subsidization

I-O sector	Industry	Absolute amount million DM		Producer subsidy equivalent(a) "s" percent	
		1974	1984	1974	1984
		traded goods			
1,2	Agriculture, forestry, fisheries	10769	20216	22.2	28.0
6-8	Mining	2094	5676	10.0	16.3
6	coal mining	1913	5528	10.7	18.2
7,8	other mining	181	148	5.8	3.2
	Manufacturing	6476	13482	0.7	0.9
	intermediate goods				
9	chemicals	562	1081	0.5	0.6
10	petroleum Refining	154	193	0.3	0.2
12	rubber goods	96	217	0.2	0.2
13	stone goods	25	32	0.4	0.5
16	iron and steel	129	2009	0.3	3.9
17	non-ferrous metals	97	136	0.6	0.5
18	foundries	43	51	0.5	0.4
19	drawing mills, cold rolling mills	40	73	0.2	0.2
30	wood	26	61	0.3	0.6
32	pulp, paper, paperboard	43	38	0.5	0.2
	investment goods				
20	structural engineering, rolling stock	114	163	0.7	0.7
21	mechanical engineering	747	1819	0.8	1.2
22	electronic data processing equipment	240	154	2.6	0.6
23	road vehicles	275	899	0.4	0.5
24	shipbuilding	242	614	3.9	8.4
25	aircraft, aerospace	643	727	17.9	8.6
26	electrical engineering	1203	1971	1.3	1.3
27	precision mechanics, optics, watches	91	214	0.7	1.0
28	metal products	145	276	0.5	0.6
	consumer goods				
11	plastic products	96	217	0.6	0.6
14	precision ceramics	24	57	0.9	1.3
15	glass and glass products	35	78	0.5	0.7
29	musical instruments, toys, sporting goods, jewellery	18	39	0.4	0.5
31	wood products	78	157	0.3	0.4
33	paper and paperboard products	63	186	0.5	1.0
34	printing	282	511	1.9	2.0
35	leather, leather goods, shoes	12	26	0.2	0.3
36	textiles	123	175	0.4	0.5
37	clothing	94	137	0.5	0.6
38,39	food and beverages	601	962	0.5	0.5
40	tobacco	116	242	0.9	1.3

Table 6 - continued

I-O sector	Industry	Absolute amount		Producer subsidy equivalent(a)"s"	
		million DM		percent	
		1974	1984	1974	1984
		nontraded goods			
3,4,5	Electricity, gas, water	513	1072	1.0	0.7
41,42	Construction	252	741	0.2	0.4
43,44	Retail and wholesale trade	616	1343	0.1	0.1
45,46,48	Transportation	13234	19053	17.0	13.4
45	railways	10055	14325	56.2	66.9
46	water transport	638	776	6.0	5.5
48	other transport	2541	3952	5.1	3.7
47	Communication (Federal Post Office)	497	2283	2.0	4.8
49,50	Banking and insurance	1081	2202	1.7	1.5
49	banking	736	580	1.7	0.6
50	insurance	345	1622	2.0	4.1
52-55	Other private services	4232	12311	2.6	3.1
52	hotels and restaurants	283	407	0.9	0.7
53	education, research, publishing	836	1802	3.7	3.2
54	health and veterinary services	2164	6906	8.3	12.4
55	miscellaneous private services	949	3196	1.2	1.4
1-55, exc.51	Business sector	39764	78379	1.8	2.0
	Coefficient of variation	.	.	2.498	2.558

(a) Subsidy divided by gross output.

Source: Calculated from Statistisches Bundesamt [h]; see Table 5.

33. Now all the ingredients for calculating effective rates of assistance have been assembled. First, however the rates of effective tariff protection alone are calculated, and displayed in Table 7. They show no surprises. In Table 8, then, the vectors of effective implicit and explicit tariff protection, effective subsidization, and their sum, the effective rate of assistance are shown (1). The pattern of protection which

_____

(1) Partial results covering most of the industrial sector have been previously published in Weiss [1988] and Donges, Schmidt et al. [1988]. The vectors of effective explicit and implicit tariff protection (EIT 1978 and 1985) underlying all these calculations are *identical*. They are published here for the first time because it had been feared that the eventual inclusion of the additional NTB's in agriculture, food, and beverages would radically change the results. Their inclusion changed only the two sectors themselves much. Effective

Table 7 - Effective Rates of Tariff Protection in West Germany (Corden Method)

I-0 Sector	Industry	1978	1985
	Manufacturing		
	intermediate goods		
9	chemicals	16.2	9.8
10	petroleum refining	10.7	10.7
12	rubber goods	12.7	8.0
13	stone goods	8.7	6.1
16	iron and steel	9.9	9.7
17	nonferrous metals	12.1	11.2
18	foundries	11.6	7.6
19	drawing mills, cold rolling mills	7.7	6.1
30	wood	21.7	16.1
32	pulp, paper, paperboard	19.3	14.2
	investment goods		
20	structural engineering, rolling stock	4.8	3.1
21	mechanical engineering	2.6	1.6
22	electronic data processing equipment(a)	8.1	9.8
23	road vehicles	10.3	12,7
24	shipbuilding	- 7.1	- 1.2
25	aircraft, aerospace(b)	15.6	14.1
26	electrical engineering	8.6	5.1
27	precision mechanics, optics, watches	7.2	5.2
28	metal products	7.9	5.7
	consumer goods		
11	plastic products	15.8	7.1
14	precision ceramics	7.3	5.6
15	glass and glass products	10.6	7.8
29	musical instruments, toys, sporting goods, jewellery	8.3	8.9
31	wood products	12.7	6.5
33	paper and paperboard products	27.9	19.8
34	printing	2.0	0.9
35	leather, leather goods, shoes	9.2	7.2
36	textiles(c)	18.9	13.3
37	clothing	31.4	23.2

(a) Own input tariffs set at zero. - (b) All input set at zero. - (c) Agricultural input implicit tariff set at zero.

Source: Calculated from Table 4 and from Statistisches Bundesamt [d] and [i].

Table 8 - Effective Rates of Assistance in West Germany (Corden Method)

I-O Sector	Industry	mid-1970's			mid-1980's		
		EIT + (1978)	ES = (1974)	ERA	EIT + (1985)	ES = (1984)	ERA
				traded goods			
1,2	Agriculture, forestry, fisheries (a)	296.8	201.1	497.9	149.0	198.6	347.6
6-8	Mining						
6	coal mining	70.3	38.7	109.0	200.2	116.5	316.70
7,8	other mining	- 4.1	16.7	12.6	- 4.0	6.0	2.0
	Manufacturing						
	intermediate goods						
9	chemicals	15.1	2.0	17.1	8.6	2.4	11.0
10	petroleum refining	10.7	5.7	16.4	10.7	5.0	15.7
12	rubber goods	11.7	2.9	14.6	7.0	3.8	10.8
13	stone goods	7.8	0.3	8.1	4.9	0.3	5.2
16	iron and steel	- 3.1	1.0	- 2.1	40.8	24.4	65.2
17	non-ferrous metals	10.8	3.6	14.4	9.4	2.8	12.2
18	foundries	10.6	1.3	11.9	4.4	1.0	5.4
19	drawing mills, cold rolling mills	7.7	0.4	8.1	- 2.0	0.6	- 1.4
30	wood	21.5	1.8	23.3	15.7	2.9	18.6
32	pulp, paper, paperboard	18.4	2.1	20.5	13.1	1.2	14.3
	investment goods						
20	structural engineering, rolling stock	4.8	2.1	6.9	- 1.3	1.7	0.4
21	mechanical engineering	2.6	2.2	4.8	0.6	3.1	3.7
22	electronic data processing equipment(b)	8.0	5.8	13.8	9.1	2.1	11.2
23	road vehicles	10.0	1.3	11.3	10.7	1.8	12.5
24	shipbuilding	- 7.2	9.8	2.6	- 4.7	24.6	19.9
25	aircraft, aerospace(c)	15.6	45.0	60.6	14.1	20.8	34.9
26	electrical engineering	8.6	3.7	12.3	4.8	3.4	8.2
27	precision mechanics, optics, watches	7.2	1.6	8.8	5.1	2.3	7.4
28	metal products	7.8	1.5	9.3	2.7	1.7	4.4
	consumer goods						
11	plastic products	15.2	1.8	17.0	6.5	1.9	8.4
14	precision ceramics	7.2	1.7	8.9	5.5	2.8	8.3
15	glass and glass products	10.4	1.4	11.8	7.6	2.4	10.0
29	musical instruments, toys, sporting goods, jewellery	8.1	1.0	9.1	8.5	1.3	9.8
31	wood products	11.9	0.9	12.8	5.7	1.3	7.0
33	paper and paperboard products	27.4	1.9	29.3	19.5	3.7	23.2
34	printing	2.0	3.9	5.9	0.8	4.5	5.3
35	leather, leather goods, shoes	8.7	0.5	9.2	6.8	0.9	7.7
36	textiles(d)	55.5	1.9	57.4	48.0	2.4	50.4
37	clothing	84.0	2.5	86.5	71.0	2.8	73.8
38,39	food and beverages	47.6	3.6	51.2	31.2	3.1	34.3
40	tobacco	124.0	26.2	150.2	124.0	37.1	161.0
				non-traded Goods			
3,4,5	Electricity, gas, water	-40.6	2.0	-38.6	-46.4	1.9	-44.5
41,42	Construction	- 5.5	0.4	- 5.1	- 4.5	0.8	- 3.7
43,44	Retail and Wholesale Trade	- 2.4	0.7	- 1.7	- 2.1	0.8	- 1.3
45,46,48	Transportation						
45	railways	- 5.9	64.5	58.6	- 6.1	100.0	93.9
46	water transport	- 7.4	20.3	12.9	- 6.6	23.3	16.7
48	other transport	- 4.8	14.8	10.0	- 4.3	10.3	6.0
47	Communication (Federal Post Office)	- 1.9	2.7	0.8	- 1.8	7.1	5.3
49,50	Banking and insurance						
49	banking(e)	-	-	-	-	-	-
50	insurance	- 2.5	4.8	2.3	- 2.1	10.2	8.1
52-55	Other private services						
52	hotels and restaurants	-23.5	2.2	-21.3	-20.6	1.6	-19.0
53	education, research, publishing	- 7.1	10.3	3.2	- 5.5	8.5	3.0
54	health and veterinary services	- 3.1	11.7	8.6	- 2.4	20.1	17.7
55	miscellaneous private services	- 3.0	1.8	- 1.2	- 2.4	2.4	0.0
	Coefficient of variation	2.75	2.67	2.59	2.62	2.40	2.33

EIT = Effective Implicit Tariff Protection; ES = Effective Subsidization; ERA = Effective Rate of Assistance. - (a) Inputs at world prices approximately equal value added at world prices. Implicit nominal protection rates just above actual rates yield negative effective protection. - (b) Own input tariffs set at zero. - (c) All input tariffs set at zero. - (d) Agricultural input implicit tariff set at zero. - (e) Due to write offs, banks' intermediate inputs approximately equal gross output. Effective rate estimate unstable.

Source: Calculated from Tables 4, 5 and 6 and from Statischisches Bundesamt [d; i].

emerges reveals some notable features, both over time, and in comparison to tariff protection alone. (Agriculture, food and beverages, and tobacco were left out of the tariff calculations to begin with because it was
expected that meaningless results would emerge if the NTB's were not
included.) Only a handful of industries really benefit from the protection
and promotion system. These are:

- agriculture, forestry, fisheries

- coal mining

- iron and steel

- shipbuilding

- aircraft, aerospace

- textiles and clothing

- food and beverages

- tobacco

- railways, and

- health and vetinary service.

The usual mercantilist protective structure is still distinctly noticeable in
the various raw material processing chains, but the levels of protection
that these industries (e.g. wood, pulp, wood products) receive is
dwarfed by those industries protected by NTB's. It is also quite remarkable how two parts of the steel complex are treated in such different
ways: the NTB's in steel caused effective protection in cold rolling mills

---

subsidization (ES), calculated as the volume of subsidies (Table 6)
divided by EIT net value added was cleaned up for 1974, and up-
dated from 1982 to 1984. The absolute subsidies for 1974 used here
differ slightly from those used heretofore. Moreover, net value
added figures inadvertently referred to 1972 in the previous calculations. The results of the changes are minor except in petroleum refining and aircraft, where value added fluctuated widely in the early
1970's. Hence, the effective rates of assistence shown here for 1974-
1978 are almost identical to those given previously. In the coal
mining sector clerical errors were corrected. Implicit nominal protection in steel, to which many sectors are highly sensitive, was left at
zero in 1978, even though it had risen to 17 percent by that year,
to reflect the "pre-Tokyo Round" levels of protection that prevailed
in the early to mid-1970's better.

to become negative, and except for the compensation through subsidies, negative in structural engineering. The one upstream industry that received enough subsidies to overcompensate for the steel NTB was shipbuilding. As with textiles and clothing, all this essentially amounts to support for declining industries. There is hardly a sign of a policy for promoting successful or potentially successful industries by means of subsidies. Electronic data processing could perhaps have been so characterized in the mid-1970's, but certainly no longer. The only other beneficiary in the industrial sector is aircraft and aerospace, and that is essentially subsidization of one product – the Airbus. Possible causes and consequences of this pattern of protection will be analyzed in the coming chapters.

III. The Coherence of Subsidization Policy

34. Subsidization policy is gradually becoming the more significant part of overall German trade policy, as was shown in the last chapter. Tariffs are changed infrequently and have been declining generally. Nontariff border measures tend to be temporary, and if not, the industries protected or promoted by them tend to be the ones subsidized as well. In addition, subsidies can be changed at the national level fairly easily from year to year. For this reason, subsidization by itself is subjected to some scrutiny in this chapter. The aim is to find characteristics of subsidization policy, or a typology of subsidies, that remain relatively stable. Firstly, the overall pattern of subsidization policy is briefly described, along with the sources of financing. Then, the interindustry evolution of subsidization policy is analyzed, comparing announced policy intentions with the actual distribution of funds. Finally, a typology of subsidization is forwarded which draws upon some durable features of the German subsidization system. Throughout, an answer is sought to the question whether a coherence in subsidization policy can be found. It turns out that such coherence is hard to find.

1. The Overall Pattern of Subsidization Policy

35. Subsidies increased noticably through the 1970's (Table 5). After the first oil-price crisis several programs were introduced which were meant to foster the restructuring process of the German economy. These programs expired at the beginning of the 1980's and subsidization policy stabilized at a higher level. After 1981 subsidies increased again. In June 1982 the Federal Government introduced a large, temporary, cyclically motivated investment-bonus program which cost DM4.1 billion in 1984 and DM2.2 billion in 1985. After the change of government in October 1982, various forms of tax relief (e.g. for agriculture and housing) were introduced, which resulted in decreased tax revenues of about DM7 billion in 1984. Moreover, and this was a break in trend, the government started to subsidize the iron and steel industry to a much

Table 9 - Subsidies Classified by Type, 1973-1984

Type of subsidy	1973	1974	1980	1981	1984
	percent distribution				
Tax exemptions					
tax rate reductions	6.0	5.9	5.3	6.0	9.0
personal and material tax exemptions	7.9	7.9	9.3	9.3	9.1
tax base reductions	16.9	16.7	15.1	15.0	17.3
Financial assistance					
debt service	4.0	4.3	3.8	3.1	2.9
current transfers	45.9	44.9	46.4	46.7	44.9
capital transfers	17.0	17.8	17.5	17.3	14.3
preferential loans(a)	2.5	2.4	2.5	2.6	2.4
	DM billion				
Total	56.9	62.3	102.7	103.0	120.0
(a) Subsidy equivalent.					

Source: See Table 5.

greater extent than before. As far as the Common Agricultural Policy (CAP) is concerned, its expenditures are meanwhile increasing such that the whole system of agricultural support might become financially unviable. Altogether, from 1981 to 1984 subsidies rose by an annual rate of 5.2 percent whereas total government spending increased by 2.7 percent [Jüttemeier, 1984].

36. Governments provide a large range of subsidies. For important subgroups, the sums are shown in Table 9. There are basically two forms a subsidy can take - tax exemption and financial assistance - with numerous variations within each form. Tax relief constitutes lost government revenue; this accounts for roughly one third of the total volume of subsidies, the biggest part consisting of deductions of certain items from the tax base (e.g. specific write-off regulations). Financial assistance

Table 10 - Subsidies Classified by Financial Source, 1973-1984

Sources of financing	1973	1974	1980	1981	1984
	percent distribution				
Tax exemptions					
personal and corporate incomes tax	16.5	16.8	17.6	17.9	22.5
property and local business tax	1.6	1.4	1.8	1.6	1.4
value added tax	9.2	9.1	8.1	8.5	9.7
other taxes	3.2	3.2	2.2	2.2	1.8
Financial assistance					
parafiscal funds(a)	0.5	0.6	3.0	2.7	2.7
common agricultural policy (CAP)	6.0	5.9	7.8	6.7	7.7
federal budget(b)	33.6	32.3	29.8	30.0	27.3
länder budgets	25.7	26.6	25.0	25.1	22.7
local budgets	3.7	4.0	4.7	5.1	4.2
	DM billion				
Total	56.9	62.3	102.7	103.0	120.0
(a) European Recovery Prgram (ERP) Fund and Coal Equalization Fund. - (b) Labor Office included.					

Source: See Table 5.

stands for cash-transfers from public budgets. By far the most important single item consists of current transfers.

37. One of the more striking features about German subsidization policy is its pronounced decentralization. Table 10 shows the institutional setting for the main sources of both tax exemptions and financial assistance. But the picture is more complex because at each government level nearly every ministry is involved in the process. The central government, for example, consists of 17 ministries, each granting some kind of assistance. Moreover, there are many state-owned credit institutions, whose task is to assist governmental subsidy policy by granting preferential loans [Jüttemeier, Schatz, 1983].

38. When it comes to the assignment of responsibility and policy formulation, however, the role of the Federal Government is by far the most important. Beyond its own budget, central government has a significant influence on the level and structure of other authorities' subsidies as well:

- Programs of the parafiscal funds are executed outside the federal administration, but the Federal Minister of Economic Affairs determines their volume and structure (1).

- The annual budgets of the Labor Office, which include for present purposes make-work programs with and without sectoral targets, are approved by the Federal Government and are supervised by the Minister of Labor.

- The volume and structure of the CAP of the EC are fixed by the Minister of Agricultural Affairs and his colleagues from other member countries. Note that CAP expenditures constitute less than half of subsidies to agriculture (cf. Table 6).

- With regard to tax policy, the constitution of the Federal Republic provides that most taxes are levied cooperatively between the federal and state levels. Nevertheless, experience shows that there are rarely any cases of tax exemptions which were not initiated at the federal level. The system of taxation and exemption is largely a federal matter.

- Fiscal federalism is not consistently adhered to on the expenditure side of budgets either. Apart from cooperative duties enumerated in the constitution (Gemeinschaftsaufgaben), the Federal Government often

---

(1) The ERP (European Recovery Program)Fund is a special property of the Federal Government. Its assets originally stem from Marshall aid granted to Western European countries after World War II. While the German Federal Government repaid the aid in US dollars by 1961, private recipients of US deliveries had to make DM payments to the Federal Government. Thus, the ERP Fund represents the DM countervalues of US aid, and is today a revolving fund. In 1952 the assets of the ERP Fund accounted for roughly DM5 billion and at present for about DM10 billion. The fund is at the disposal of the Federal Government and it is used mostly for structural adjustment policies. The Coal Equalization Fund which in public is better known as "coal penny" is financed through an extra levy on the consumption of electricity. The revenues are used to subsidize the input of domestic coal in electric power plants.

Table 11 - Subsidies Classified by Government Functions, 1973-1984

Government functions	1973	1974	1980	1981	1984
	percent distribution				
General public services	0.9	1.0	1.2	1.4	1.3
Educational, cultural, religious affairs	7.9	8.4	8.4	8.6	8.3
Social security and welfare	23.2	23.6	21.7	23.0	21.3
Pollution abatement and control affairs	0.4	0.3	0.4	0.4	0.6
Civil and military research	7.7	7.7	7.7	8.0	7.8
Regional policy	8.5	8.7	7.8	8.3	7.9
Sectoral policy	51.4	50.3	52.8	50.3	52.9
	DM billion				
Total	56.9	62.3	102.7	103.0	120.0

Source: See Table 5.

gets state governments to participate in special federal subsidy programs (subject to approval of the Bundesrat (Upper House)), such as in the program for coal, steel, shipyards, and countercyclical and general structural measures.

On the whole, cautious calculations indicate that the Federal Government is directly responsible for roughly four fifths of all subsidies [Jüttemeier, 1984, pp. 36 ff.].

39. The volume of subsidies may be regarded as an index manifesting the perceived correction requirements of the government. Table 11 shows the main fields of operation grouped according to the UN classification system of government functions.

- The biggest part is spent for sector-specific programs, like agriculture, coal mining, the iron and steel industry, shipyards, all means of transportation, and tax relief for public banks.

34

- The social security function comprises a variety of measures such as general employment schemes of the Labor Office and the promotion of new small businesses but also selective aid programs for farmers, miners, construction workers, tenants, and to private nonprofit institutions. (The figures in the table exclude non discriminatory schemes.)
- The amounts of regional and research related programs are roughly equal. Both policy functions often provide subsidies in sectorally rather unspecific ways.

Over the years, the shares of the different functions do not vary much. Due to new programs, however, sector-specific programs (agriculture, steel) have increased significantly since 1981.

2. The Interindustry Pattern of Subsidization

40. Breaking down subsidies by broad sectors (Table 12) reveals that the service sector receives most subsidies (roughly one third) while subsidies for the goods producing sector are increasing most. But nominal, and (approximately) effective subsidization in the goods producing sector is dwarfed by agriculture and housing. And, while the share of money going to agriculture declined, the rate of subsidization increased substantially. In 1984 subsidies for the service sector amount to DM4 410 per employee and DM14 650 for agriculture, but only DM2 010 for the goods producing industries (Table 12).

41. For all that, the extent of promotion or discrimination within the goods-producing sector is not uniform, and more importantly, has changed over time (see Table 8). Coal mining, the iron and steel industry, and shipbuilding stand out as having received a much larger share of subsidies in 1984 than in 1974. The share going to modern industries, particularly aerospace and electronic data processing, but also fissionable materials, subsumed under chemicals in the table, fell. Four fifths of the total volume of subsidies originate in budget items

Table 12 - Subsidies to Four Broad Economic Sectors, 1973-1984 (percent)

Sectors	1973	1974	1980	1981	1984
Agriculture					
share	18.3	17.3	16.7	14.9	16.8
producer subsidy equivalent(a)	21.7	22.3	26.8	22.8	27.9
subsidy/value added(b)	45.2	50.8	77.8	68.8	79.7
subsidy/person engaged (DM)	5410	6150	11940	10800	14650
Goods production					
share	15.1	14.9	16.5	16.8	17.5
producer subsidy equivalent(a)	1.1	0.8	1.0	1.0	1.1
subsidy/value added(b)	2.4	2.5	3.2	3.3	3.6
subsidy/person engaged (DM)	670	760	1460	1530	2010
Services					
share	32.0	31,6	31.9	31.7	31.0
producer subsidy equivalent(a)	1.9	1.9	2.0	1.9	1.9
subsidy/value added(b)	8.4	7.7	7.9	7.3	7.0
subsidy/person engaged (DM)	2270	2460	3880	3860	4410
Housing and nonprofit institutions					
share	34.6	36.1	35.0	36.6	34.7
producer subsidy equivalent(a)	24.1	24.7	24.2	23.5	21.1
subsidy/value added(b)	46.1	47.5	49.7	48.9	42.2

(a) Subsidies/gross output at domestic prices. - (b) At domestic prices.

Source: See Table 5.

which were conceived for a single enterprise or branch of industry; only nine percent originate in broad based schemes out of which 25 or more industries obtain benefits [Jüttemeier et al., 1977].

42. Noteworthy is especially the development of subsidization of the iron and steel industry. Until the end of the 1970's, the steel industry only occasionally received some assistance out of broad-based schemes. In 1978, however, the Federal Government and the government of the Saar gradually started to subsidize the ARBED-Saarstahl Company to a large extent by means of a so-called restructuring program for steel mills of the Saar area. Meanwhile, subsidy programs covering all steel companies came into existence. From 1974 to 1984 the steel industry's subsidies increased almost twentyfold, thus exceeding the average growth of subsidies in the economy as a whole (Table 5 and 6).

36

There are also a few branches which can be regarded as the sprinters. In the aircraft and aerospace industry the degree of subsidization fell significantly and for data processing, assistance even decreased absolutely. Remarkable is the decline for data processing since it is one of the rare cases where the Federal Government suspended its sector-specific program due to the failure of the policy of "picking a winner". The reasons for previously granting assistance were typical for infant industries. Even though they received large sums of assistance, the subsidized computers did not succeed in the market place, and the Federal Government finally altered its policy towards a more broadly-based innovation policy.

43. Does the German Government pursue an industrial policy, consciously or unconsciously, then? An examination of policy pronouncements suggests not. At least, the normative objectives of policy positively observed are often difficult to discern. The law underlying the Federal Government's biannual report on subsidies prescribes that for every program, policy objectives have to be listed. Actually, the objectives mostly consist of descriptions of instruments, assessment bases, or the legal regulations under which subsidies will be granted. In numerous cases they simply say "cost reductions for agriculture", "improvement of earnings and liquidity in coal mining", or even more simply state "promotion of air transport", "of savings behavior", "of showmen's business", or "social considerations", or "good for public welfare". By and large, it seems that the grantors of subsidies do not really know themselves what overall social or economic goals they are striving for, at least not on a coherent basis. In the recent past, some of the largest programs (e.g. agriculture, coal mining, housing) are described as sacrosanct matters of constitutional norms [Deutscher Bundestag, c, p. 11], a description which sounds quite defensive.

44. Remaining at the level of pronouncements, something more coherent can perhaps be said about policies towards individual industries (1). In sectoral policy, emphasis is placed on two broad principles. Firstly, as-

(1) Cf. Deutscher Bundestag [b], which dates from 1968 but is still referred to today as a declaration of principles of sectoral policies.

sistance is to be given to increase productivity and promote economic growth. Secondly, problem industries are to receive assistance in reducing capacity and avoiding the social problems associated with employment reduction in declining industries. Promotion of the aircraft industry, data processing and nuclear energy fit in with the first goal, and subsidies for shipbuilding, coal, and steel seem to follow from the second goal. In addition, some element of maintaining a national strategic energy reserve can be discussed in policy towards the coal industry. Agricultural policies are said to be based on the Treaty of Rome, and a corresponding national law of 1955. However, neither the Rome Treaty nor domestic law requires subsidies, let alone the specific subsidy policy actually carried out.

45. Regional considerations form another rationale for subsidization. Since West Germany is a federation made up of eleven states and a high degree of consensus among the states and the Federal Government is constitutionally required, regional interests play a substantial role in policymaking. Apart from some sectorally broad-based programs, the territorial extension of which is limited to structurally weak regions and West Berlin, a lot of sector-specific schemes might be interpreted as a special kind of regional policy as well. Coal mining and the steel industry play a dominant role in the Ruhr and Saar areas, shipyards are concentrated in four coastal states, and aircraft in Bavaria, Bremen, and Hamburg. Agriculture is still important for some less developed areas in some federal states, and quite often the Federal Railways are required to maintain uneconomic routes there. There is always an incentive among the states to "haul ashore" benefits for industries located on their territory: receiving gifts, even if they are not in optimal form, improves welfare.

46. Summarizing the comparison between policy pronouncement and policy practice, one can fairly say that there is no coherent concept or systematic guideline behind subsidy policy. Normally, several distributional and allocational goals are pursued simultaneously. In spite of a high focus of subsidization programs on individual branches and even enterprises, a consistent set of sectoral selection criteria seems to be absent. German subsidization policy, probably like that of most other countries, appears

as the sum of a wide range of ad hoc measures. Moreover, such criteria as can be found tend to change over time.

3. Subsidies and Policy Institutions

47. Somewhat more light can be shed on the actual motives for subsidization if one classifies subsidies according to the (roughly stable) institutions which grant the transfers. One can usefully distinguish among:

- research and development (R&D) policy;

- regional policy; and

- sectoral and ad hoc policy.

This classification is useful because the bulk of R&D subsidization (80 percent in manufacturing) is carried out by one ministry - the Federal Ministry of Research and Technology, albeit within the framework of a large number of direct and indirect promotion programs (of which a small number are large). The bulk of regional subsidization is carried out by a special joint federal state body which sets up regional and industrial criteria for granting aid to businesses. There is no intention of discriminating against particular sectors here. In addition, a "Zonal Border" Promotion Program targets aid to regions bordering the GDR. In fact, two thirds of the surface of West Germany containing one third of its population qualify. Finally, the separate budgetary and tax aids to West Berlin should be subsumed under this heading. The sectoral policy measures are the ones based on separate laws enacted in the Bundestag and the state parliaments on an ad hoc basis, whereas there is more central direction in R&D policy and more continuity in regional aid.

48. The volume of these three types of subsidies is shown in Table 13 for the early 1980's.

- Programs to promote research activities constitute one important source (30 percent) of subsidies in manufacturing. The government prefers financial assistance to individual projects framed for specific industries and products (direct promotion), while tax relief for general activities (indirect promotion) is of minor importance. The sectoral pattern certainly specifies nearly all branches as recipients of research aids, but actually only very few of them receive appreciable amounts (mechanical as well as electrical engineering, aircraft, fissionable materials power). Moreover, there is further intrasectoral concentration: a small group of the largest German manufacturing companies absorbs most funds. For 1974 figures are available showing that 13 big companies obtained 70 percent of all such research aids to manufacturing industries which were provided by the Federal Ministry of Research and Technology (80 percent) [Jüttemeier et al., 1977, p. 174].

- The most important source of subsidies to manufacturing industries are general programs which are meant to promote regions. Such programs incorporate West Berlin, and an area along the border to the GDR and Czechoslovakia, as well as other regions which have a per capita income very much below the average of the Federal Republic. Regional promotion is rather broad-based, that is to say, there are few regulations concerning the exclusion of certain industries from regional-related assistance. However, the sectoral distribution of such subsidies suggests that there is a slight bias towards capital-intensive branches.

- At the beginning of the 1980's, sectoral policy schemes were still of minor significance (19.9 percent). Only shipbuilding, aircraft, iron and steel, and fissionable materials power benefitted to any extent. Allocating public funds to aircraft and nuclear energy is part of a policy to pick the winners, while assistance for shipyards and the steel industry is part of the maintenance of declining industries and unprofitable firms in order to avoid immediate sacrifices for the labor force. Since shipyards and steel companies are still under heavy competitive pressure from abroad, and since their regional concentration is very high, the Federal Government and the respective state governments have intensified their programs substantially since then.

Table 13 - Subsidies by Policy Institutions, 1980/81 (percent)

I-O Sector	Industry	R&D Policy	Regional Policy	Sectoral Policy
			traded goods	
1,2	Agriculture, forestry, fisheries	0.1	0.1	99.8
6-8	Mining	6.2	0.7	93.1
6	coal mining	5.8	0.3	93.9
7,8	other mining	19.2	19.8	61.0
9-40	Manufacturing	29.4	50.7	19.9
	intermediate goods			
9	chemicals	29.6	51.9	18.5
10	petroleum refining	15.8	26.9	57.3
12	rubber goods	20.0	80.0	0.0
13	stone goods	11.3	78.1	10.6
16	iron and steel	34.4	29.8	35.8
17	nonferrous metals	31.9	45.9	22.2
18	foundries	18.8	70.8	20.4
19	drawing mills, cold rolling mills	29.4	64.7	5.9
30	wood	5.8	82.7	11.5
32	pulp, paper, paperboard	10.8	67.6	21.6
	investment goods			
20	structural engineering, rolling stock	21.7	75.9	2.4
21	mechanical engineering	60.7	33.4	5.9
22	electronic data processing equipment	70.8	28.5	0.7
23	road vehicles	21.1	75.8	3.1
24	shipbuilding	13.7	4.8	81.5
25	aircraft, aerospace	48.9	1.3	49.8
26	electrical engineering	38.5	60.9	0.6
27	precision mechanics, optics, watches	27.9	49.7	22.4
28	metal products	13.9	83.9	2.2
	consumer goods			
11	plastic products	15.0	83.3	1.7
14	precision ceramics	16.3	76.7	7.0
15	glass and glass products	14.6	79.2	6.2
29	musical instruments, toys, sporting goods jewellery	16.1	83.9	0.0
31	wood products	11.0	83.9	5.1
33	paper and paperboard products	3.8	93.1	3.1
34	printing	2.0	30.3	67.7
35	leather, leather goods, shoes	17.4	65.2	17.4
36	textiles	12.5	85.2	2.3
37	clothing	5.7	93.5	0.8
38,39	food and beverages	2.5	88.9	8.6
40	tobacco	0.0	95.7	4.3
			nontraded goods	
3,4,5	Electricity, gas, water	14.7	24.2	61.0
41,42	Construction	7.2	67.9	24.9
43,44	Retail and wholesale trade	0.0	95.7	0.3
45,46,48	Transportation	0.3	1.3	98.4
45	railways	0.0	0.1	99.9
46	water transport	1.4	2.2	96.4
48	other transport	1.1	5.3	93.6
47	Communication (Federal Post Office)	0.0	4.8	95.2
49,50	Banking and insurance	0.1	5.3	94.6
49	banking	0.3	10.9	88.7
50	insurance	0.0	2.3	97.7
52-55	Other private services	5.1	10.7	84.2
52	hotels and restaurants	0.3	94.5	5.2
53	education, research, publishing	11.1	13.4	75.5
54	health and veterinary services	0.1	1.8	98.1
55	miscellaneous private services	13.7	16.2	70.1
1-55, exc.51	Business sector	6.0	12.3	81.7

Source: See Table 5.

4. Subsidies and Factors of Production

49. Another typology whose elements could exhibit some stability are subsidies to factors of production; at least some of the announced aims of policy could be achieved by subsidizing factors of production. Table 14 shows the interindustry breakdown of subsidies by recipient factors;

- German subsidization policy is marked by the preference given to physical capital. Almost 40 percent of all subsidies to the business sector promote fixed capital formation in some way. Methods include the promotion of entrepreneurial income formation (tax base reductions for farmers and self-employed professions, tax exemptions on dividends, interest payments, and rents); the compensation of deficits (railways); and equity capital formation (in coal mining, railways, communication, and small and medium-sized enterprises).

- Labor income related subsidies are generally of minor importance. Some sector-specific programs, for instance, favor agriculture (takeover of social security contributions by the Federal Government), coal mining (wage-bonus for pit miners), and construction ("bad weather pay"). Sectorally broad-based programs exist for R&D-related personnel and for employees working in West Berlin.

- An increasing share of subsidies is assigned to gross output promoting sales or maintaining high domestic prices or compensating for them. Subsidy programs intended to reduce sales prices are available for exports from West Berlin to the other parts of the Federal Republic (reduced rates of value added tax), for specific goods and services (e.g. reduced rates of value added tax for books and medical service, preferential treatment of the income tax for some kinds of insurance contracts) or for new ships and planes. Maintaining high prices is the main duty of the CAP; it is also given for coal mining through deficiency payments to electric power plants (Coal Equalization Fund) and to the iron and steel industry (consumption of domestic coke). Other product related payments concern subsidies to German ship-owners, if their ships are built in German yards.

- Intermediate inputs are favored through a wide range of measures. This is especially true for most R&D programs of the Federal Ministry for Research and Technology but also for most promotion of private

Table 14 - Subsidies by Factors of Production, 1980/81 (percent)

I-O Sector	Industry	Output	Inter-mediates	Labor	Capital
		traded goods			
1,2	Agriculture, forestry, fisheries	48.7	7.7	3.1	40.6
6-8	Mining	37.2	19.1	21.5	22.3
6	coal mining	38.0	18.7	21.9	21.4
7,8	other mining	2.9	26.2	12.4	58.5
9-40	Manufacturing	24.4	16.8	15.4	43.3
	intermediate goods				
9	chemicals	14.5	12.9	10.7	61.9
10	petroleum Refining	0.6	46.3	0.7	52.4
12	rubber Goods	7.8	5.1	18.4	68.6
13	stone Goods	6.0	4.2	13.1	76.7
16	iron and steel	6.3	21.3	9.0	63.4
17	nonferrous metals	30.2	13.0	7.7	49.1
18	foundries	10.6	7.3	20.4	61.7
19	drawing mills, cold rolling mills	10.5	12.4	25.2	51.9
30	wood	5.8	2.2	6.4	85.6
32	pulp, paper, paperboard	5.6	2.2	9.1	83.1
	investment goods				
20	structural engineering, rolling stock	26.7	8.1	16.2	48.9
21	mechanical engineering	7.1	15.4	23.6	53.9
22	electronic data processing equipment	9.8	39.3	33.0	17.8
23	road vehicles	2.6	6.4	11.9	79.1
24	shipbuilding	60.7	18.5	9.5	11.3
25	aircraft, aerospace	6.0	42.5	30.3	21.1
26	electrical engineering	29.5	18.4	29.1	22.9
27	precision mechanics, optics, watches	44.7	10.7	25.1	19.5
28	metal products	40.7	3.0	17.1	39.1
	consumer goods				
11	plastic products	8.4	4.7	14.0	72.9
14	precision ceramics	0.0	6.0	13.5	80.4
15	glass and glass products	0.0	6.9	10.3	82.8
29	musical instruments, toys, sporting goods, jewellery	33.9	2.2	18.1	45.8
31	wood products	3.9	3.2	9.4	83.4
33	paper and paperboard products	15.8	1.1	8.1	75.0
34	printing	74.2	0.5	6.2	19.1
35	leather, leather goods, shoes	23.8	6.4	12.7	57.1
36	textiles	15.7	4.9	14.7	64.7
37	clothing	56.2	2.9	12.8	28.1
38,39	food and beverages	45.8	2.0	7.1	45.0
40	tobacco	68.1	0.0	7.6	24.3
		nontraded goods			
3,4,5	Electricity, gas, water	3.1	7.7	4.5	84.9
41,42	Construction	10.3	2.0	30.4	57.3
43,44	Retail and wholesale trade	46.1	0.5	19.9	33.5
45,46,48	Transportation	8.3	22.1	31.6	38.1
45	railways	2.3	11.7	48.8	37.3
46	water transport	0.1	44.1	0.8	54.9
48	other Transport	31.6	23.9	6.6	38.0
47	Communication (Federal Post Office)	5.5	0.6	2.4	91.5
49,50	Banking and insurance	63.9	0.0	3.4	32.8
49	banking	0.2	0.0	6.0	93.8
50	insurance	97.4	0.0	2.0	0.6
52-55	Other private services	49.7	11.9	9.2	29.3
52	hotels and restaurants	1.8	1.4	10.5	86.2
53	education, research, publishing	7.1	18.5	12.9	61.5
54	health and veterinary services	75.8	7.4	5.8	11.1
55	miscellaneous private services	23.5	18.5	16.1	42.0
1-55, exc.51	Business sector	31.0	15.7	14.1	39.2

Source: See Table 5.

nonprofit institutions. Selected inputs, on the other hand, are subsidized through tax exemptions from excise taxes (e.g. gasoline).

50. In most cases rather small amounts of money are involved. Subsidies
are of minor significance for most branches; only a few industries are
subsidized to a great extent. This becomes obvious again when comparing subsidies in relation to the aggregates subsidized. Thus, there is no
evidence for any prevailing overall strategy of channeling public assistance to branches by means of subsidizing different aggregates. Rather,
it seems that some highly subsidized industries performing comparatively
poorly, like agriculture and coal mining, are assisted more than average
through all channels.

51. The promotion of investment is the main goal, particularly for most
manufacturing industries, which together obtain 43 percent of their subsidies for investment activities (Table 14). Roughly 10 percent of total
investment of the private economy is financed through assistance out of
public budgets. Since the German tax system is often said to be less at-
tractive for capital formation than those of other countries [cf., e.g.,
King, Fullerton, 1980], the orientation of German subsidization policy
towards investment promotion might be regarded as a corrective. However, the intersectoral pattern of selective investment assistance does
not give much evidence for subsidization policy stepping in as a pro-
mising substitute for general tax measures: there is a negative rank-
order correlation to be observed between the ratios of investment promotion of the different industries and their long-term economic performance (growth rates of real gross value added) which is strongest for the
subgroup of highly subsidized industries ($r = -0,61$). Thus, investment
promotion proves to be mainly a device for maintaining less successful
industries.

5. Conclusion

52. A number of points characterizes German subsidization policy:

- The main institutional feature of the system is marked by its large scattering and decentralization. Subsidies are distributed from roughly 10 000 different budgetary items in the federal and other budgets.

- The large number of programs may give the impression that many different objectives were pursued by the authorities. However, neither the logic of economic goals and the ranking of their priorities is clear, nor is there coordination among different grantors of subsidies. A coherent industrial policy all of a piece does not exist. At the level of policy pronouncements a commitment to a growth-oriented subsidization strategy is most consistently made.

- The package of subsidy programs has something in store for everyone. Actually, each industry receives some kind of assistance, but only very few branches receive remarkable amounts. Multiple subsidization from different suppliers and programs for the same purpose and activity is quite often observed.

- From the interindustrial pattern of the distribution of subsidies there is no evidence for an exclusive subsidization strategy of picking the winners. More indications point to an overall strategy of maintaining less successful industries, especially, since the biggest part of all subsidies is spent for some declining industries. Subsidies are supported to do a bit of everything, which contributes to the policy's incoherency.

The complex and confusing system favors tendencies to look at it from a partial point of view, i.e. the promotion of one product, one enterprise, one region, or one production-line, and since many programs contain rather small sums of money the issue of financing subsidies is mostly not taken into account or is played down as a negligible fact at the margin.

IV. The Political Economy of West Germany's Trade Policy

53. How can one explain why the mixture of industries receiving increasing or continuing high support from economic policy was benefitted? As the discussion of subsidization showed, there is apparently no coherent centrally-directed industrial policy operating in West Germany. Changes in tariff policy, in turn, were not hammered out in national isolation, but through international negotiations, intermediated of course through the EC. Nontariff border measures are mostly, but not strictly, unilateral. Nevertheless, there is something systematic happening in the policymaking process. Trade policy outcomes can be explained by the interaction of a small, distinctive, and stable set of interest groups with a limited number of stable and distinctive German, European or international institutions. The "political economy of protection" framework perhaps goes further in explaining changes in present-day German trade policy than for other countries with a more fragmented set of interest groups, such as the United States, or a still more encompassing set of interest groups, such as Sweden, because of this distinctiveness.

54. The politico-economic approach to trade policy specifies an economic logic considering the costs and benefits to private agents in lobbying for, or demanding protection, and to governments in granting, or supplying protection. While the framework is plausible enough, it is often difficult to predict results for the pattern of trade policy because the constraints facing agents, or the costs and benefits they incur, are hard to specify. Clearly, the constraints facing agents, though not their objectives, are to large part determined by the political system. Political institutions are similar enough in western countries to warrant application of a general politico-economic approach, but relevant details do differ across countries. The salient institutions which have been identified in determining the demand for and supply of protection are elections and political parties [Downs, 1957; Brock, Magee, 1978]; the extent and size of interest groups [Olson, 1965; 1982]; the degree of acceptance of an ideology [North, 1983]; the power and structure of bureaucracy [Tullock, 1965; Niskanen, 1971; Messerlin 1981]; and the state of international relations [Borchardt, 1984].

While it is easy to list the factors affecting the level and structure of protection, it is sometimes hard to specify precisely how they affect demand and supply, as Caves [1972] discussed. For example, in a single member district election system to the representative body, an industry concentrated in a single district will have an incentive to lobby for increased protection in the face of adversity. Whether the industry is successful depends upon the constraints on log-rolling imposed by political parties or the representative body. Industry representatives know this. Will demand be higher or lower in such cases? More to the point for the German case, the supply side of the political economy approach is often modeled along the lines of a median voter model with two parties competing for power [Brock, Magee, 1978]. But the potentially severe influence of coalition politics has been left out of the picture. Well organized groups are likely to have lower transactions costs in framing a common platform for lobbying. Under normal circumstances such groups are likely to be small, following the logic of Olson [1965]. This severely circumscribes the number of votes which can be mobilized in an election. Ideology is also not easy to handle. According to North [1983], ideology is a device for lowering transactions cost. Thus, it has a positive influence on both demand and supply of protection. If the role of ideology is to be tested, and not merely assumed, one would have to examine the cost of eliciting protection directly; quantity information alone would not suffice. Similar problems apply to analyzing the influence of bureaucracy. Strict application of the Downs-Niskanen vision of the bureaucracy would suggest greater protection in sectors overseen by a bureaucracy because this leads to more for the bureaucracy to do. But bureaucracies are confronted with incentives the rulers make, and if the rulers are free-trade oriented, presumably such bureaucrats will achieve pecuniary and nonpecuniary rewards who are successful in implementing the rulers' vision (1).

Finally, it should not be forgotten that foreign economic policy is foreign policy, as well as economic policy. How governments react to interest groups demanding protection, or free trade for that matter, depends on

---

(1) See the example of the Prussian bureaucracy, discussed in the next chapter.

the political leadership foreign policy interests. This has been cogently argued by Borchardt [1984]. In an economic analysis of the causes of protection, this could be treated as affecting the costs of eliciting protection.

55. Some of these indeterminacies can be resolved with the help of a perception by Waelbroeck [1986]. In Europe, at least, organizations are in place and functioning. There is no free rider problem inhibiting the effectiveness of lobbying groups. This applies even more to the situation in West Germany, as will be shown below. These organizations are in place, and often large, but not always so large as to make them so "encompassing" in the sense of Olson [1982] that they take account of the social costs of their dysfunctional behavior and hence promote free trade.

The same results from an application of Messerlin's [1981] views on bureaucracy to the case of West Germany. Messerlin essentially applies Olson's conception of the encompassingness of organizations to the bureaucracy. If a bureaucrat has widely divergent interests to administer, he will be more free-trade inclined, essentially because he has to take account of the deleterious consequences of granting one sectional interest's demand for protection on other sectional interests.

56. Something not considered in the political economy literature so far, but quite relevant to the German case, is the establishment of policy automata. This means that support programs have been taken out of the political sphere proper and are adjusted according to previously determined criteria, according to some prespecified formula. In such cases, agents are even further removed from the awareness of any budget constraint, and protection can spiral under the given formula. Two such institutions exist in West Germany, one for a particular industry and one for a large slice of support policy. Here, too, Olson's views on encompassingness are vindicated. The narrower interest has received increased protection, and the broader-based support policy has been less distortionary, but in turn, has lost out in the competition for resources.

57. While consideration of European, or particularly German institutions goes a long way to make this positive theory of the political economy of protection operational, it throws cold water on an attempt to quantify an important normative aspect of the process. Early on, it was recognized that lobbying activity directed at eliciting protection would increase estimates of the cost of protection by orders of magnitude [Krueger, 1974; Tullock, 1967; Bhagwati, 1982; Robert E. Baldwin, 1982]. The reason is simple: private agents would invest in lobbying activities until the rate of return from that activity equalled the competitive rate of return on productive economic activity. Measurement of the deadweight losses resulting from lobbying would have to be added to the static losses from protection. Such quantification, Waelbroeck [1986] pointed out, would be practically impossible for Europe because organizations were founded long ago, in the nineteenth century, and the investments they made were not in measurable physical capital, but often in the form of personal and human sacrifice, as in the founding of trade unions. Thus, the economic rationale for, and the social costs of lobbying are made difficult to test by these institutions, but they do aid in operationalizing the positive theory of political economy for the case of West Germany (1).

1. Interest Groups and Institutions in Manufacturing

58. At first sight, the existence of the observed special beneficiaries of trade protection is difficult to square with widely-held beliefs about trade policy making institutions and the pattern of interest groups in West Germany. The country is strewn with a somewhat encompassing set of organized interest groups, which find equally encompassing counterparts in government. Under such conditions, according to Olson [1982], one would expect relatively efficient policy outcomes, that is to say free trade. The reason is that large groups, were they to seek benefits at

---

(1) Magee [1987] reports simulation experiments of the social cost of lobbying. It seems that lobbying can turn the economy into, as he puts it, "a black hole".

the expense of outsiders through imposition of distortions, would themselves bear a substantial share of the social cost of such measures.
Hence, they will refrain from lobbying for such measures.

59. Indeed, the bulk of manufacturing does come under a liberal trade
regime. All of West German industry is organized in one large organization, the Bundesverband der Deutschen Industrie (BDI - Federation of
German Industry). This association is organized along branch lines,
i.e., each industry has its own component organization. Important examples are the "Verein deutscher Maschinenbau Anstalten" (VDMA) for the
machinery industry, the "Zentralverband der Elektrotechnischen Industrie" for the electrical equipment industry, and Gesamtverband der
Textilindustrie for clothing and textiles. The peak association represents
industry as a whole vis-à-vis the government bureaucracy on all issues
of interest to it, decidedly including foreign trade policy. Issues of work
and pay, however, are left to another all-encompassing organization, the
"Bundesverband deutscher Arbeitgeberverbände" (BDA - Federation of
Germany Employers). Each individual industry of course promotes the
policies it favors, but there is a fairly large degree of coordination at
the top of the BDI through its Außenwirtschaftsausschuß (Foreign Trade
Committee) on which all member industry organizations are represented.
The position of the BDI on trade policy is as one might expect - free
trade is a good thing. Because some members are under pressure from
lower cost sources of supply, the BDI tolerates special-trade policy
measures in their favor, but as exceptions to a general rule.

60. Another encompassing organization, which is important beyond the
mere weight of numbers, is the "Deutscher Industrie- und Handelstag"
(DIHT - German Chamber of Industry and Commerce), the modern relic
of the guild system. Its membership comprises one third to one half of
all craftsmen and tradesmen. The significance of the DIHT arises from
its para-state activities, e.g. in setting standards and examinations in
vocational education; it is thus as much a state institution as a lobby.
Since its members do not compete directly with imports (bakers, plum-
bers, electricians) it is decidedly pro free trade, and articulates this
position in public.

61. The government counterparts of these organizations in respect to trade policy are all to be found in the Ministry of Economics. This Ministry contains industry desks, and of course a certain amicability between these and the corresponding particular industry organizations cannot be denied. But the industry desks are all in one department, whereas other departments (Außenwirtschaftspolitik - Foreign Economic Policy) and particularly the "Grundsatzabteilung" (Basic Principles Department) take the broad view. And, of course, there is the broad view which emerges at the top of the Ministry. All of this is entirely consistent with the hypothesis of Messerlin [1981], that the wider the area of responsibility of a bureau the more it will tend towards free trade. In West Germany, at least, even the internal departmental structure reflects the desire to generate "the broad view".

62. It is the Economics Ministry which represents West German economic policy interests to the European Commission in Brussels, so that this broad view - for the bulk of manufacturing industry - gets tabled there. Indeed, the BDI also does its broad-view lobbying directly to the Commission in Brussels. On matters of trade policy for the bulk of manufacturing, no other German ministry has any substantive say, not even the Ministry of Finance, though all interested ministries are formally involved in interministerial committees on every measure at every level, and the Ministry of Foreign Affairs is titular head of any international negotiations or treaties.

63. The situation is entirely symmetrical on the labor side. German labor unions are highly encompassing organizations organized along branch lines with a powerful enough center, the "Deutscher Gewerkschaftsbund" (DGB - Federation of German Labor Unions), though perhaps its power is waning, and the branch unions are gaining at the expense of the top (1). The largest individual union is the metal workers union (IG Metall), with 1 500 000 members in 1985, purportedly the world's largest. This union, as well as the central organization, knows that jobs depend on exports in the highly open German economy. As late as 1982, an anti-protectionist article appeared in the DGB's scientific journal [Kühne,

(1) See Göbel [1988] for an overview of the postwar German union movement and evidence for this decay of central authority.

1982]. Thus, one cannot say that the union movement is protectionist. Individual unions, such as the clothing workers, might be, but the movement as a whole certainly is not. Protectionist tendencies at the industry level will be tolerated as "exceptions" much as the BDI tolerates them. On the other hand, a protectionist industry association can expect effective support from the corresponding union.

64. German unions enjoy influence far beyond a mere reflection of their membership size. They negotiate pay scales and working conditions for all employees in an industry, members and nonmembers alike [Soltwedel, Trapp, 1987]. They effectively negotiate minimum wages, for union rates are regularly validated by the state governments and become statutory. There is no closed shop, and union organizations are in place, so nonmembers enjoy an effective free ride if they find employment at the legal wage. Not least because of the quasi-automatic validation of union pay scales by state governments, unions, like other really encompassing organizations in West Germany, are as much pillars of the state as they are lobbies.

65. The encompassingness of institutions which are to deal with the great bulk of manufacturing at the government level even in a formally federal governmental structure is illustrated well by the way in which regional aid is handled. This form of aid amounted to 30 percent of all subsidies received by manufacturing industries in 1980, so that the illustration is quantitatively significant. The single largest program of regional aid is the Joint Federal State Program (Gemeinschaftsaufgabe des Bundes und der Länder) to improve the regional economic structure, half financed by the states, half financed by the federal government. The program is one institutionalization of a constitutional policy to equalize living standards across West German regions.

66. Aid is distributed to individual regions (rather than to specific industries) based on criteria determined by the Federal and state governments jointly through a Planning Commission (1). This has an idiosyn-

_____

(1) The criteria agreed upon proxy per capita income, provided there is an industrial base of some kind. A brief description of the criteria used is given in Adlung et al. [1979, pp. 171-179].

cratic voting procedure: each state has one vote, but the Federal government has votes equal to the sum of the number of states. Furthermore, a three-fourths majority is required to carry a proposal. But this institutional set-up implies that individual state interests can easily be stymied: while an industry concentrated in one state may lobby at the state level, and that state may very well desire granting that industry regional aid, that state would have to overcome the opposition of all the other states, as well as the federal government. State votes could surely be traded, but a majority could never be achieved that way. Given perfect trading among states on each issue, the federal votes still constitute a blocking coalition.

67. The issues decided in the Planning Commission within the framework of this program are the specification of towns and cities, along with some of their environs as potential "pôles de croissance", eligible for receiving direct subsidies, reduced interest loans, and loan guarantees on industrial investment undertaken there. The subsidization base is capital investment. Noteworthy about the outcome of this procedure is that there is very little discrimination between regionally-concentrated and unconcentrated industries on account of the blocking of the log-rolling process. Furthermore, while there is a bias toward the promotion of capital intensive industries, there is no conscious selection of specific industries (1).

2. Features of the Highly Protected Sectors

68. Given these sorts of institutions, one would not expect much discrimination among sectors of economic activity. Yet, the analysis in Chapter II showed that the variation of effective rates of protection in-

---

(1) The second major regional aid program aims at maintaining the economic viability of West Berlin. The subsidy base is similar to that of the Joint Federal/State Development Program, namely investment. But this program does not really promote regionally concentrated industry, as West Berlin's economic structure still corresponds quite well to that of the dozen or so other major German cities.

creased from the mid-1970's to the mid-1980's. If one reviews the list of highly favored industries (agriculture, food processing, coal and steel, shipbuilding, aerospace, and textiles and clothing), all save shipbuilding and textiles and clothing fall completely outside the encompassing institutional framework outlined above which applies to manufacturing industry: agriculture and food processing are matters for the EC, as are coal and steel. In addition, coal mining is in effect a nationalized industry. Except for steel, but in addition to textiles and clothing, they have been taken out of the formal jurisdiction of the GATT by international agreement. Agriculture and food processing explicitly, and aerospace implicitly have their own ministries. In addition, agriculture has its own established lobby, der Deutsche Bauernverband.

a. Coal and Steel

69. The coal and steel industry fall completely outside the encompassing institutional structure extant in the bulk of manufacturing. Tellingly, these two industries received special treatment because of the state of international political relations, aided and abetted by the ideology of European unification prevailing just after the Second World War. In the immediate aftermath of the war, the western allies directly controlled German steel and coal output (International Authority for the Ruhr). The French proposal - the Schuman Plan - to maintain control of the European coal and steel industries jointly, was seen by the Federal Republic both as an easing of the occupation regime generally and a chance at regaining international prestige [Harbrecht, 1984, p. 13]. For this reason, and because accession to the Schuman Plan ameliorated French designs on the Saar, the West German government welcomed the Schuman Plan and signed the treaty of the European Coal and Steel Community (ECSC), which became effective in July 1952. This policy was of course completely consistent with Adenauer's policy toward France [Feld, 1981, p. 33]. In fact, it is difficult to claim that much national authority was delegated to the new High Commission. Internal trade barriers came down, and external tariffs, but not other instruments, such as import quotas, were harmonized by 1958.

70. By that time imported oil was becoming cheaper, and the cost difference between American coal and domestic coal was growing. The response
of the by then EC member states was different enough to prevent the
emergence of a common coal policy [Swann, 1984, p. 246 ff.]. Italy has
almost no domestic coal production and had become a large importer of
petroleum. It was interested in a low coal price and a low oil price. Consistent with a divergence of national interests, and the power invested
in the High Authority, a coal support program consisting of national
financial measures, granted by the Authority as exceptions to the prohibition on most kinds of aids embedded in the ECSC treaty, was promulgated. It was financed nationally. In 1966, permission was granted to
national governments to subsidize coking coal down to the world level to
prevent new locations for steel making activity from becoming economic.
Thus even exports to EC member states may explicitly be subsidized.
Clearly, German steel was a great beneficiary of this program. The
mixed strategy that was implemented in the 1960's has been maintained in
its essential features to the present day.

It consisted mainly in (1):

- subjecting coal imports from non-EC countries to binding quantitative
  import restrictions;

- assuring, by means of subsidies and compensation payments, coal consumption on the two markets essential for it - coke supply in the steel
  industry and furnace coal used in electricity generation; and

- adapting output capacities of the domestic coal mining industry to market perspectives.

The latter indeed resulted in a reduction of extracting capacity from
150 million tons per annum by the end of the 1970's, to about 90 million
tons at the beginning of the 1980's.

71. The automatum built into protection results from a combination of the
first two elements. The steel industry was, of course, against border

---

(1) The following three paragraphs draw on Neu [1986]. See also Fels
    and Neu [1980].

protection of coke. So as not to tax the steel industry, an "Iron and Steel Contract" was worked out in 1966 (amended in 1985) to the effect that the steel industry promised to use exclusively German coke, but that it would receive a subsidy equivalent to the difference between world market price and domestic price. In addition, such a subsidy is paid on coal exported to EC countries, so that steel industry relocation in the Amsterdam-Rotterdam-Antwerp region, where coal could be cheaply imported on account of low transport costs, for purposes of exporting to West Germany, was made uneconomic (1). As the discrepancy between German production costs and world market prices have increased, the subsidies have soared. The 1985 change in the Contract foresees quantity ceilings on coal eligible for subsidization.

72. Institutional arrangements for furnace coal use in electricity generation are similar, in that a portion of domestically-used coal is subsidized down to the world market price. In another contract, the domestic electricity generating industry agreed to buy fixed annual quantities of coal (47.5 million tons by 1985) under these conditions. In addition, some liberalization of import quotas is foreseen.

73. Steel, like coal and agriculture, came under EC auspices (2). As in agriculture, there was no legal necessity to intervene to preserve the industry. As in coal, the first common measures taken may be see as responses to short-term business cycle problems: in contrast to coal, where a re-nationalization of policy was allowed to develop, steel policy from a very early stage was community policy. Perhaps the policy was a common one, because European steel firms had long experience in trying to work together in their Eurofer cartel.

74. The first steps of the European Commission were harmless enough. In 1963 tariff and nontariff protection against imports from third countries was increased in response to a "temporary decline in sales". These were renewed from year to year and, in 1967, a voluntary export re-

(1) These subsidies are to be phased out by 1991.
(2) The next four paragraphs draw on Dicke [1987] and Herdmann, Weiss [1985].

56

straint was negotiated with Japan. Throughout this period, the commission promoted the steel industry with financial assistance designed to increase capacity.

75. By the mid-1970's, minimum prices for steel products were being promulgated and export restraints negotiated with third countries. National subsidization policies were beginning to proliferate. By 1980 a "crisis" was apparent, and the detailed regulation of the steel market became earnest. As in coal, Commission's role was not so much to distribute money to the member countries' steel industries, but to regulate how the subsidies were to be granted. Production quotas were introduced, presumably so that the subsidies - which are essentially transfers to cover companies' losses - don't get out of hand. Since the early 1980's import quotas - negotiated and imposed - have been tightened.

76. For all that, the German steel industry is to an extent at least, a victim of these measures. It is probably the lowest cost producer in the community, as its industry representatives claim (1). Therefore, it benefits from foreign trade protection, but is prevented from increasing exports to the other EC countries. Indeed, the industry has come out in public demanding an end to production quotas and subsidies, and the German government opposed the initial introduction of production quotas. Furthermore, direct financial assistance to cover losses has only been received by one German steel company.

77. Summarizing the coal and steel experience, it might be appropriate to say that the center - the Commission - doesn't make any policy. Rather, it makes rules all member states can live with, and imposes the least common denominator of external protection. This last all community members acquiesce in. If they do not, as the case of coal in Italy shows, then no common external policy is made. Measures above the least common denominator tend to get financed by national governments, with the Commission keeping a watchful eye on measures so that they do not end in too strong a policy competition, as shown by the case of steel.

----

(1) See also World Bank [1987].

b. Agriculture

78. The agricultural sector clearly illustrates the primacy of politics in external economic policymaking. The economic order which emerged mirrored the balance of French and German agricultural interests (1). France was willing to form a customs union for industrial products only if an agricultural union was established at the same time. Other potential signatories to the EEC treaties, particularly the United Kingdom, feared that high agricultural tariff countries, like Italy, would work to raise the initial common agricultural tariff, thereby reversing a low price policy oriented to consumers, and undermining Commonwealth preferences. Aside from having different initial levels of protection for agriculture, various potential members of the EEC had different structures of protection, as well. France and Italy had export surpluses in grains, Holland in meat. It was clear that the establishment of a CAP was going to require sharp changes in each countrys' internal price structure and would hence affect various interest groups noticeably. For this reason, and because the common policy was going to be carried out by a supranational agency, most OECD countries refused to join. Only the six countries already organized in the ECSC assented.

79. Interestingly, the Treaty of Rome did not prescribe the type of agricultural policy to be followed. It left open three possibilities:

- common competition rules;

- international policy coordination; or

- common, binding pricing policies.

Somewhat paradoxically, France, the low agricultural price country, insisted on long-term contracts at guaranteed prices. West Germany would have preferred mere international policy coordination, even though the existing German agricultural regulation system was highly dirigiste. The French saw the danger of surpluses at a raised price level; the Germans saw the high cost (potentially to them) of exporting their price level and structure. The compromise that emerged was perhaps the worst possible.

---

(1) The next two paragraphs draw on Dicke et al. [1987].

Important goods' prices would be set in common (grain, pork, eggs, poultry, wine, beef, milk and sugar); the costs of agricultural policy would also be borne in common, and the prices were subject to negotiation.

80. The setting of common prices, along with common intervention in key products, financed in common, nourish the belief that a common agricultural policy actually exists. This is by no means the case, however [see, e.g., Davenport, 1980]. Soon after the implementation of the common policy began in 1967, the French franc was devalued (in 1969). So as not to exacerbate already apparent surpluses, the implied FF price increase was not passed on to French farmers in full. In the same year, the new upvaluation of the Deutsche mark was accompanied by widespread farmers' protests at having to accept the implied cut in prices [Feld, 1981, p. 69]. Thus, the monetary compensation amounts, isolating each national economy's farm prices from the Community became institutionalized. Such export levies and import taxes still exist, though they vary from year to year [Swann, 1984, pp. 222 f.].

81. These national price differences, together with purely domestic financial assistance formalized at the time of the initial Franco-German compromise on the price of wheat, the lynch-pin of the agricultural price structure, support the view that the agricultural price cum subsidy policy prevalent in each country is in fact a national matter [see, e.g., Marsh, Swanney, 1983, p. 60]. As in the case of coal and steel, it seems to be the least common denominator of any nation's policies that gets institutionalized, with individual countries free to add on extra benefits to particular constituent groups.

82. Nonetheless, separate ministries and lobbies, and international agreements probably do not suffice to explain the great power of German farmers vis-à-vis their own government to first influence and then add on to community agricultural support. Of course, the lobbying and ministerial constellation is identical across European countries in the case of agriculture. And the field of agriculture is one of the few in which an effective European-wide lobby has emerged - Committee of Professional Agricultural Organizations, COPA [Philip, 1983, p. 22; Michelmann,

1981, p. 155]. These tend to emerge where the Community is strong, in agriculture it is strong only relative to other areas of policy activity, and not in the sense of determining the vast bulk of policy measures carried out in any one member country. Instead, the common strength of farmers in Community countries seems to result form the nature of coalition politics in many European countries. Farmers and their interest groups exploit their power to swing governments. Farming groups seem to be large enough to matter at elections and cohesive enough to deliver the vote. Fitzmaurice [1983] identifies this situation in France, where there is competition for farmers support among groups on the right, in Denmark and even in Britain at times. This widely held view [see also Henig, 1979] apllies to West Germany a fortiori, because of its destinctive political spectrum.

83. On the whole, German farmers, like all farmers, are fairly conservative people, so that the initial level of protection farmers received prior to the founding of the EC may be said to correspond roughly to their relative power in the Christian Democratic Union (CDU), the conservative party. Indeed, new aid to farmers during the 1960's, when the CDU was senior partner in government, consisted of social welfare benefits, such as subsidized pensions (Höcherl Plan). Since the farm population was shrinking, this was an economically-efficient, eventually self-liquidating subsidy program. It was also politically efficient - the CDU as a large encompassing organization wanted no truck with supporting an interest group whose members were going to vote CDU anyway and which could only impose costs on the rest of its supporters. The Social Democratic Party (SPD) and the Trade Unions (DGB) had always been for low farm prices [Feld, 1981, p. 51].

84. Things changed fundamentally after the 1969 general election which led to a coalition government with the SPD as senior partner and the Free Democrats (FDP) as junior partner. The FDP was always in danger of falling below the 5 percent of the vote required to enter the Bundestag. It wanted, and received the Ministry of Agriculture, and promptly went fishing for new voters to keep the party over 5 percent of the vote. Economically, each extra vote had an extraordinarily high value to it. By the same token, the SPD stood no chance of ruling alone, and the

FDP was its only possible coalition partner. The value to the SPD of an extra vote for the FDP was thus also extraordinarily high. Hence the senior coalition partner readily acquiesced in a transfer in the form of higher food prices and taxes from its supporters, the workers, to the farmers, who voted more for the FDP than previously. It has been said that the Ministry of Agriculture was virtually autonomous during this era [Fitzmaurice, 1983, pp. 4-5; Michelmann, 1981, p. 158].

85. The change in government in 1983 did not bring back the coalitional structure of the 1960's. A relatively stable left-right split means that the three coalition partners have no alternative to each other, but one of the coalition partners, the Christian Social Union (CSU), the Bavarian wing of the CDU, again depends heavily on farm support. Thus not only do the farmers have a lobby, they also have a client party and a client state government. In addition, farmers are no longer an intramarginal group to the coalition as a whole. They express their resentment by staying away from the polls, as in the elections to the Bundestag in 1987. This led to an overproportional rise in the agricultural budget since 1983 - while the central budget rose by 6 percent the agricultural budget climbed by 33 percent from 1984 to 1987. Nevertheless, the "Deutsche Bauernverband" presented a catalogue of 50 new demands for the next legislative period [FAZ, 1987]. Lest the cause of the resentment be misunderstood, the nature of EC farm policy makes the resentment legitimate. Price supports essentially increase the rent accruing to intramarginal (large) farms. The many small farms, as in Bavaria, perceive only costs. But the many small farms have more votes than the few large ones. Put differently, the farmers' lobby has been representing the interests of the larger farms rather than the small farmers. Even a new small-farmers interest group has been founded, the Bauernbund. It engages in anti-lobbying actively against the established Bauernverband, and now competes with it in elections to governmentally-supported cooperative enterprises and institutions. This shift in the structure of interests, or even perceptions, means that possibly a lever can be found to change German farm policy, and by extension EC farm policy in the near future. Relevant for the political economy point of view is that aside from the availability of more information for farmers as voters, the party currently responsible for the Ministry of Agriculture, the CSU, is on the

one hand a much more encompassing organization qua party than the FDP is, and on the other closely tied to a still larger party, the CDU. For ideological reasons it doesn't have the room for swinging coalitions the FDP has. Most recent indications do point to a slight change in German farm policy, at least at the margin. Early pension benefits to farmers, coupled with land consolidation, are being expanded [Handelsblatt, 1988].

c. Shipbuilding (1)

86. As in coal and steel, protection for the shipbuilding industry started during the late 1960's, as a measure against what was seen as cyclical unemployment. On the other hand, that protection has endured is at least partly attributable to the regional concentration of the industry. The four coastal states, in which shipbuilding is concentrated (Bremen, Hamburg, Lower Saxony and Schleswig-Holstein) later took up the cudgels for the industry, both at the federal level and with their own support programs.

87. The first severe recession after World War II in West Germany in 1967 brought about unemployment, which in retrospect appears moderate. But it was concentrated in the mining districts and some coastal regions. The Federal government created a program to support investment, in which the four coastal states participated. Under this program, yards received subsidized credits if investment was undertaken for building big ships, new types of ships, or for introducing new production techniques. This program did not remain the only state intervention in investment in the shipbuilding industry. Contrary to their original intention, regional programs, which were meant to promote a wide range of activities in specific regions, were used intensively to promote the shipbuilding industry. Furthermore, the states became joint proprietors of big yards in Kiel, Hamburg and Bremen.

---

(1) This section draws on Lammers [1984].

88. In 1976, capacity utilization of German yards declined sharply. Orders of oil tankers and bulk carriers had already dropped as a result of the first oil crisis and the world recession in 1974. Especially those yards that were supposed to have specialized on promoted types of ships were hit. In response, ships exported to LDC's were declared "development assistance projects". Furthermore, the Federal Ministry of Research and Technology set up several R&D programs for the yards. Also, the Ministry of Defence ordered new ships earlier than originally planned and in deference to the employment problems of the large yards accepted substantial extra costs. But the decline of production and orders could not be stopped, and yards reduced their work force: the number of employees shrank from 73 thousand in 1975 to 59 thousand in 1979.

89. An "Auftragshilfeprogramm" (Direct Building Subsidy Program) was in operation from 1979 to 1981. Only the construction of special vessels was subsidized; oil tankers and bulk carriers were excluded. When the Federal Government refused to participate in financing a second direct building subsidy program, the coastal states decided to run such a program on their own. But the interventions in favor of the shipbuilding industry could not prevent large yards from running into severe difficulties. AG-Weser at Bremen closed down at the end of 1983 and the remaining yards at Bremen were merged with substantial financial support from the State of Bremen. The state of Schleswig-Holstein covered losses of Howaldtswerke Deutsche Werft AG, the biggest German shipyard, located in Kiel and Hamburg; capacities for the building of new ships were closed at Hamburg and reduced at Kiel.

90. The story of subsidization to the shipbuilding industry is remarkable in the sense that state governments not only took up the lobbying initiative at the federal level to obtain more funds as competitive pressures increased, but also stepped in with their own resources. The Federal government had aided the states, but not so much as necessary to ward off substantial employment cuts. Regional concentration of an industry is apparently hardly sufficient to obtain funds from central government in a federal system. The situation in shipbuilding stands in sharp contrast to the one in coal mining, which is also regionally concentrated, even more

than shipbuilding, but the federal government essentially took on the role of supporting the industry. Party politics cannot be used to explain the outcome. At the beginning of the coal support programs, the federal government was ruled by a different party than ruled North Rhine-Westphalia, and throughout the shipbuilding support regime the four coastal states were ruled by various parties.

d. Textiles and Clothing (1)

91. International restraints on the textile and clothing trade generally predate World War II. As tariffs and restrictions came down generally after the war, bilateral restraints were negotiated by West Germany with Japan, India, and Pakistan in the 1950's. It was at the same time that the US desired the restriction of Japanese exports of cotton textiles to its domestic market. The textiles industry was the first to become competitive in the developing countries, and had benefitted from quite high protection in the industrialized countries. Cline [1987, p. 146] describes the actions taken at that time as "initiating a cycle that has plagued textile protection ever since: the spillover from controlled to uncontrolled areas". Numerous other bilateral restraint agreements were negotiated by West Germany within the multilateral framework provided by the STA (Short-Term Arrangement Regarding International Trade in Cotton Textiles) from 1961 to 1962 and the first two phases of the LTA (Long-Term Arrangement Regarding International Trade in Cotton Textiles), 1962-1967 and 1967-1970 respectively. The import restrictions had two characteristics in common: they covered only cotton products and they were negotiated by West Germany rather than by the EC. The latter changed in 1970, the year the LTA was extended for the second time: the EC officially took over commercial trade policy for all of its members, thereby causing a gradual phase-out of previously negotiated bilateral agreements starting in 1971. The import restraint agreements subsequently negotiated by the EC were characterized by global EC-wide quotas that were distributed among member countries according to some unwritten principle of "burden sharing", a principle carried over to the MFA of 1974

---

(1) This section draws on a manuscript by Zietz [1986].

and its four extensions in 1978, 1982, and 1986. Starting with LTA III (1970-1973) it became clear, however, that several national quota allocations were rather low compared to domestic demand thus leading to a diversion of imports that legally entered the EC in one member country to the more restrictive countries. Reacting to this undercutting of import restrictions from within the Community, France and the Benelux countries stand out in that they have frequently resorted to Article 115 of the EEC treaty. In practice this has meant that they obtained the authorization not to apply Community treatment to products in free circulation in other member states. (The trade in domestically produced substitutes cannot be restrained, however.) In contrast, West Germany has been among the EC countries using the most restraint with regard to Article 115 (1). In fact, in 1973, still under LTA III, the German government even requested a substantial increase in West Germany's EC quota allocations.

92. Starting in 1974, import protection in clothing and textiles took on a new dimension with the introduction of the MFA and its four subsequent prolongations. First and foremost, the MFA has meant an extension of protection to fibers other than cotton, initially to synthetics and wool (MFA I), but eventually to all fibers that are of any use for mass marketing in clothing and textiles (MFA IV). Secondly, the country coverage of import restrictions was greatly expanded so that by the middle of the 1980's almost all exporting countries with the notable exception of industrialized countries are subject to nontariff export restrictions.

93. Although in West Germany some segments of the administration, in particular the Ministry of Economics, seem to be in favor of reducing protection in textiles and clothing, there are strong opposing forces at work: both unions and employers' associations as well as some fellow member countries of the EC are vigorously opposed to any lessening of the protectionist grip in textiles and clothing. This helps to explain partly the staying power of the MFA in spite of its often repeated temporary nature. The element of discrimination inherent in the MFA has added to its political appeal and staying power. Since the import re-

(1) Compare Spinanger and Zietz [1986] for details and see Table 1.

strictions are not directed against fellow industrialized countries, there is no fear among restricting countries of retaliation from a potent trading partner, an important factor normally helping to keep protection in check. In these circumstances, it is difficult to identify any significant domestic or foreign pressure that politicians who decide on protectionist legislation in industrialized countries would have to reckon with, except perhaps the People's Republic of China. On the domestic side, it seems worth bearing in mind that the agency with broad interests to defend, the Ministry of Economics, seems to be liberal-minded.

e. Aerospace

94. The German aerospace industry is the only modern sector which is heavily protected. Its effective protection stands in sharp contrast to its export orientation. The aerospace industry is special in several respects:

- due to allied prohibitions after World War II, the German aerospace industry was not rebuilt until the late 1950's.

- the German aerospace industry is to a large extent involved in cooperation programs - civil and military - in the EC;

- a large part of aerospace output, i.e. most military and space products, is sold to the government.

These combined factors led to a unique institutional structure. The industries are concentrated; today there are essentially three producers of large commercial aircraft worldwide, a few more military aircraft producers and very few engine producers. Government involvement is heavy if only because of military and security interests. Commercial markets for aerospace products are dominated by large transport aircraft which account for the largest part of turnover.

95. When the ban on aerospace activity was partially lifted in 1955 upon West Germany's accession to NATO, the first activities of the pre-1945 companies consisted of military subcontracts for the American Airforce. Also contracts with the German Ministry of Defense led to a rapid expansion of the industry; its turnover rose from DM12 million in 1957 to

DM410 million in 1961. In the early 1960's, the development of civil commercial aircrafts was financially supported by the German government. Finally, European cooperation with Airbus industries starting in the late 1960's led to a company structure comparable in size to the American competitors Boeing, McDonnell Douglas and Lockheed.

96. Heavy government involvement stems from the fact that a large part of aerospace output never enters commercial markets. The military content of the German aerospace industry has fallen from practically 100 percent in the 1960's. Mainly with the expansion in the production of Airbus the military share of industry turnover has been reduced to about 50 percent. One third of the aerospace industry's sales in 1981 stemmed from the Tornado warplane alone. Such military shares are still very high when compared to other industries, but low compared to the same industry in other countries. European space activities are still relatively small, but these R&D-intensive activities are almost exclusively financed by governments.

97. What stands out about the aerospace industry among other highly protected industries is its closeness to defense and in the case of Germany the presumption which was at least at one time reasonable that it was only a question of time and resources before international competitiveness could be regained. Therefore, one would not want to be too quick to support a "capture" theory of government institutions in this case. Initially, government ministries are often, though not always, the instruments for carrying out government policy. Only after the policy becomes less pressing are they captured. A case in point is the nationalization of the Prussian railways for clear defense reasons [Laaser, 1983]. Only in the course of time do rent seekers get to use the ministry for their purposes. Indeed, aerospace seems to be the one industry in which government support has gone hand in hand with rising international competitiveness, though this statement is weakened, in turn, by the recognition that the market for military aircraft at least, is of course a restricted one.

3. A Statistical Verification

98. Because interest groups have been practically institutionalized in West Germany, discussion of group interests, or at least interests of the group leadership, to the neglect of considerations of group organization costs in studying lobbying effectiveness, is justified. Organizations are in place, the costs of forming them having been paid in the past [Waelbroeck, 1986]. Moreover, the organizations exist along branch-of-industry lines. This makes a statistical test of these propositions quite straightforward. In contrast to more pluralistic polities, one would expect a unique direction of influence between industry employment (as a proxy for votes) and lobbying effectiveness, the usual free-rider problem in organizing groups having been overcome. Labor unions along branch lines already exist and are ready to disseminate information (ideology) to workers. Similarly, the weight of entrepreneurs in their own councils, and hence toward the government, would increase with greater employment.

99. Regionally-concentrated industries should also expect to get more assistance, from the subnational *and* national governments. While it is recognized that low organization costs for regionally concentrated industries contribute to their lobbying effectiveness in pluralist polities, like the United States, their politico-geographic isolation speaks against lobbying success. In West Germany, a high degree of consensus building, explicitly including regional aid, is a constitutional matter, and the identification of regional success or failure with the policies of a limited number of political parties, suggests that no party can afford to let a regionally-concentrated industry decline unassisted, though as discussed, the aid should not be expected to be forthcoming from the broad-based regional aid programs, but rather as special industry assistance policies.

100. Also implicit in the institutional discussion so far has been the positive role of the possibilities for transnational policy trades in reducing protection. More broadly, the role of international affairs in allowing governments to override some interest groups has been relatively neglected in the political economy literature. Borchardt [1984] cogently

argues that international relations must be taken into account to make sense of the success or lack of success of interest groups in eliciting protection.

101. Two other determinants of the structure of protection emphasized by the political economy literature can also be applied to a structured polity like West Germany's: firstly, the external motor driving interest groups to bring forth demands for protection are declines in international competitiveness. This should be no different in West Germany than everywhere else. Secondly, concentrated industries should also be more successful in driving home requests for aid, not because organizational costs are lower (organizations are in place), but because interests might be more homogeneous.

102. These ideas can be tested statistically for trade policy changes in West Germany over the period of the Tokyo Round. Proxies for all the variables save one (the international negotiating situation) are easy to find and straightforward. One can try to explain the absolute change in effective total protection (tariffs plus implicit tariffs plus subsidies) across industries (in percentage points) between 1978 and 1985 (ΔERA) by:

- voting power, proxied by the number of employees in each industry (N), definitely expected positive in West Germany;

- regional concentration, measured by the coefficient of variation of each industry's employment across the eleven Bundesländer (Reg), ambiguous, even in West Germany;

- firm concentration, measured as the market share of the six largest firms in each industry (CON6), expected posititve in West Germany;

and the change in international competitiveness and the international negotiating situation.

The change in international competitiveness (comparative advantage) of industries can be usefully proxied by Liesner's [1958] and Balassa's [1965] concept of Revealed Comparative Advantage, creating actual export and import flows as reflecting actual comparative advantage, subject to random shocks and policy biases. The change in RCA might be used to capture the driving force behind changes in effective protection. Here, however, the policy biases working actual export and import flows are the objects of explanation. Hence, in order to avoid a simultaneity problem, the causes of the change in competitiveness can be used. The factor proportions theory of the commodity composition of international trade works very well in explaining trade flows (between countries with not too similar factor endowments), provided human capital as a factor of production is somehow taken into account [Kenen, 1965] (1) in addition to physical capital and labor. In a factor proportions context, the change in competitiveness across industries over time is caused by the same determinants as the structure of competitiveness at a point in time. The reason is clear: given factor intensities of goods, only factor accumulation changes competitiveness. A country accumulating human capital faster than another will experience an increase in competitiveness in its human capital intensive goods. Of course interindustry and intercountry differences in the rate and direction of technological progress will also play a role in determining changes in international competitiveness. But there is no reason to suppose that the direction will vary across countries, or even that the rates will diverge noticeably across countries much over a seven-year period. This holds even more when a main correlate of technical process, human capital intensity, is explicitly taken into account.

Therefore, the following are included in the regression equation

- human capital intensity, proxied by wages and salaries for employee minus an unskilled worker's earnings for each industry (h), definitely expected negative in West Germany,

- physical capital intensity, proxied by the capital stock per employee for each industry (k), expected positive in West Germany,

How to include the international negotiating situation in such a regression is far from obvious. It is a particularly difficult problem for the explanation of protection changes across industries, because the (vague)

---

(1) See Deardorff [1984], for a survey of US evidence and Weiss [1983] for a survey of evidence from West Germany.

concept of negotiating situation would seem to apply to all industries as a package. Other authors have adopted the initial rate of protection in each industry to capture various aspects of the negotiating situation or of other determinants of changes in protection (1). During the Kennedy Round, for example, tariffs were to be reduced proportionately; during the Kennedy Round high tariffs were to come down proportionately more than low tariffs. The sign and size of the estimated coefficient on initial protection rate (ERA 78) would at least track to what degree intentions were fulfilled.

The following regression was run:

$$\Delta ERA = 31.38 -23.28 \ln h + 8.26 \ln k + 6.00 \ln N$$
$$(- 3.53) \qquad (2.40) \qquad (2.81)$$

$$+ 14.78 \ln Reg + 0.32 \ln CON6 - 0.47 \; ERA \; 78$$
$$(1.84) \qquad (2.93) \qquad (- 5.11)$$

$F = 8.31$; $\bar{R}^2 = 0.61$; $n = 29$; t-statistics in parentheses.

All coefficients save the one on regional concentration are easily significant at the 1 percent level and all save one (k) show the expected sign (2). In addition, experiments with a small number of alternative specifications showed that the influence of the explanatory variables is robust provided the past level of protection is included.

103. By and large, the regression vindicates the political economy explanation for trade barriers, but two issues to interpret do arise. The first, which is relatively straightforward, is the role of an industry's regional concentration in eliciting protection in a federal state. Theoretical considerations are ambiguous here. What this econometric evidence for West Germany shows is that there seems to be some weak (as shown by low precision of the estimate) tendency for regional concentration to

---

(1) Cheh [1974] and Riedel [1977] adopted this proxy, but their interpretation is different.
(2) Data sources for the regression are Table 8; Baumgart et al. [various issues]; Statistisches Bundesamt [a; c; j].

promote protection. This weakness can be viewed as the juxtaposition of nondiscriminatory broad-based regional programs with discriminatory state and national government programs. The second issue is the unexpected sign on the physical capital intensity coefficient which bears interpretation. Because both human and physical capital intensity are supposed to capture the causes of an industry's international competitiveness, and most empirical tests of the structure of trade flows show the unexpected sign on physical capital intensity, one could say that the regression is at least consistent with other such tests. If one takes the regression seriously as data analysis, though, the results are suggestive and challenging: physical capital intensity per se seems to lead to higher protection. This occurs even when industry concentration is controlled for. Nothing in the political economy literature suggests that physical capital intensity should play this role; indeed, it is difficult to think of a reason why this should be so. If the description should be correct, however, it attests to the backward focus of overall protection and assistance policy. Industries whose competitiveness at high wage locations is in serious doubt seem to get an extra measure of state aid, given all other political considerations.

104. As it stands, then, the regression equation underlines the role of the international negotiating environment in trade barrier reductions. Might this not amount to an overinterpretation or incorrect interpretation of a detected statistically significant influence of the initial level of protection? Consider how alternative hypotheses have fared. Cheh [1974] suggested that trade policy makers act to minimize short-run labor adjustment costs. At the same time he postulated that the tariff structure at any one point in time is the product of a host of historical influences, or that the tariff structure is hysteretical. Consequently, to test his hypothesis, he allowed for hysteresis by focussing on changes in the tariff structure and including the initial level of protection as an explanator of the observed change. Cheh tests his proposition on US trade barrier reductions (in percentage points) associated with the Kennedy Round of multilateral tariff cuts. Using various proxies for labor adjustment costs, the political power of an industry (total employment), and the initial level of protection to capture hysteresis, Cheh found that only total employment in each industry and the initial level of protection were

statistically significant explanators of tariff reductions, and then only for changes in nominal protection. Tariff reductions were indeed lower in initially highly protected industries. Hysteresis seemed confirmed, his own hypothesis refuted, and political power vindicated.

105. Riedel [1977] sought to test Cheh's labor adjustment cost minimization hypothesis for West Germany's (implicitly, the EC's) tariff reductions during the Kennedy Round. While Riedel took pains to replicate Cheh's econometrics, his own interpretation of the causal process was decidedly politico-economic. In contrast to Cheh's results, Riedel found no evidence for hysteresis: a quantitatively small, but statistically quite secure effect was found going in the other direction - high protective levels were reduced slightly more than low protective levels. In addition a large industry labor force and low human capital intensity made for small reductions in protection. These results suggest that what is observed may be attributable to differences in the appropriateness of various hypotheses to different countries, rather than to any fundamental flaw in Cheh's approaches.

106. More worrying for the political economy approach as a whole is the broader international comparison of econometric results carried out by Anderson and Baldwin [1981]. Both for changes in the structure of protection over time, as well as for the explanation of the structure at a point in time, some measure of unskilled or low-wage labor intensity is consistently carrying the burden of explanation in most countries. This also applies to the study for the United States' protective levels undertaken by Fieleke [1976], but not for German protective levels undertaken by Glismann, Weiss [1983] and Witteler [1986]. Other variables, especially proxies for industry concentration, switch sign from country to country, and measures of export or import performance are consistently good explanators, but are difficult to square with the underlying theory once political factors have been taken into account.

107. Additional evidence that a politico-economic logic at work in West Germany is given by Witteler [1986]. Border measures and subsidies affect organized and unorganized groups in different ways. Consumers are the least organized and least powerful, even in West Germany.

Hence, resistance to a price raising measure should be small. In contrast, price raising measures affecting inputs to businesses can be expected to evoke organized resistance. Therefore, subsidies would be the promotion instrument of political choice in such cases. A regression equation explaining the ratio of the effective rate of border protection to the effective rate of subsidization in West Germany in 1982 with a cubic function of the share of output going to consumers is easily significant at the 1 percent level of significance.

108. A comparison of the present results with those for United States tariff concessions during the Tokyo Round [Baldwin, 1985b, pp. 165-168] is also revealing. In estimating a "demand" for protection equation, Baldwin finds that the previous tariff level is positively associated with demand whereas in the final outcome (reduced form demand and supply equation) the initial level of tariffs played no role. This could mean that forces working to maintain "hysteresis" in the United States were ameliorated, but not reversed, by the international tariff-cutting process.

109. The role of the international political climate quite apart, the present results strongly support a political economy interpretation for at least part of the changes in protection in West Germany. Firstly, they confirm Riedel's results for a previous round of tariff cutting in Germany and Europe. Secondly, in contrast to the United States, a single, questionable variable is not bearing the burden of explaining changes in protection, but more of the factors suggested by the political economy approach contribute. In Baldwin's US regressions, a measure for unskilled labor intensity essentially explains tariff changes. Yet, Baldwin [ibid., p. 165] rightly points out that "Since unskilled, low-income workers are poor pressure group organizers and advocates, the significant negative relationship between these variables and the magnitude of duty cuts ... strongly suggests that demands from pressure groups based on short-run self-interest are insufficient to explain protection reductions". Similar views are also to be found in Finger et al. [1983].

While this may be true for the United States, it is decidedly untrue for Europe. Societal groups on this continent are highly organized, often on the basis of past investments in organizing activity [Waelbroeck, 1983].

Hence, the factors included in a regression equation can more readily than for the United States be associated with either the demand (interest groups) or the supply (government) sides of protection in a unique way with a unique direction of influence. Put differently, the high degree of group organization in Europe solves (almost) the identification problem.

4. Implications for the Uruguay Round

110. If the outcome of international trade barrier reduction negotiations depended upon domestic political economic or interest groups alone, one would have to be mildly pessimistic about a German contribution to that process. This would be particularly true if the kind of cross-section regression shown above were stable for all time; it is not. Still, the exogenous variables driving the change in protection are all slowly changing variables, but they do change. Important is employment, the proxy for voting power. Employment in highly protected industries has shrunk in West Germany (Table 15). Because, as was explained, political influence is highly institutionalized, mere voting power isn't everything, but it does matter. Hence, one can fairly count on some loss in power on the part of the highly protectionist interest groups. If this were the only effect at work, one would expect a desire for moderate movement towards freer trade for the great bulk of manufacturing, in line with what emerged through the Tokyo Round.

111. But the international negotiating environment plays an important role. While the possibility of a hegemonic power conceding more than necessary and thus assuming a role of leadership in moves towards freer trade is less relevant today than a generation ago, or a century ago, a large country making demands and offering concessions, like the United States today, can still promote movement. The positive demand has been the widening of the negotiating agenda to include agriculture. There is a happy coincidence with a state of flux in the German domestic interest group structure. This could allow West Germany to play a more decisive role - within the European Community - in movement towards freer trade at the multilateral negotiations. The costs of farm policy, both for the

Table 15 - Labor Force in Highly Protected Sectors in West Germany, 1960-1986 (1000)

Sector	1960	1973	1979	1985	1986 (a)
Agriculture	3581	1924	1481	1360	1344
Food and beverages	907	922	889	796	786
Coal mining	497	237	215	199	196
Iron and steel	478	350	311	233	228
Shipbuilding	95	71	58	46	43
Textiles	721	484	347	261	257
Clothing	548	444	334	251	248
Business sector	23201	22785	21382	20444	20603
(a) Preliminary.					

Source: Statistisches Bundesamt [h].

budget and in terms of votes has become extraordinarily high. EC farm policy has essentially benefitted large, i.e. intramarginal farms. Their owners are not the ones who deliver the votes. This has been meanwhile recognized by the small farmers, who have responded by staying away from the polls during the Bundestag election of early 1987, and threatening the ruling coalition. They have further founded a new farm lobby set against the entrenched Bauernverband. Tellingly, the BDI has broken its century of silence on farm policy: it, too, sees that farm policy has become too expensive [BDI, 1987]. It proposes a system of direct income supports. The mid-1980's thus present the ruling coalition government with the following situation:

- the farm vote is needed to stay in power;

- the other EC countries will not accept the demands for higher prices tabled by the German Ministry of Agriculture;

- the German federal budget cannot bear the cost of supporting farmers by supporting output prices in the present way;

- the farm lobby, propounder of past policies, is under attack from the farmers.

A particularly hard line on agriculture on the part of the United States, provided always there is a willingness to make concessions in other fields, would be quite helpful here.

112. This analysis does not overrate West Germany's influence in the EC. A resolution of agricultural trade issues cum weakening of German farmers would shift the whole balance of economic influence in the European Community toward more free trade. West Germany uses up much of its politico-economic capital in Brussels urging increased agricultural protection. The German position in agricultural policymaking in Brussels is the opposite of that for industry; it is generally the most protectionist country in the EC. If that issue were removed from the EC agenda the country could defend its free trade ideology and free trade interests far more credibly and would have to make fewer concessions to protected trade on other issues. A pronounced shift in the standpoint of the EC would have repercussions for more free trade throughout the world economy.

V. German Trade Policy in Historical Perspective

1. Introduction

113. Germany's rich and subtle tariff and trade policy history illustrates the point that a political economy of protection explanation for ordinary changes in level and structure of protection goes far, particularly during stable times, but that large swings in protection go hand in hand with major political, institutional or technological changes, usually accompanied by a different ideology. Interest groups do have an influence on protection, but they are constrained by the state. This is particularly pronounced when the state's own foreign policy interests are directly involved, as emphasized by Borchhardt [1984], but extends to major domestic upheavals as well. In Germany, such events have often, but not exclusively, been associated with the aftermath of (lost) wars.

2. The Prussian Reforms

114. The defeat of Prussia in 1806 and the Napoleonic Wars left Germany in an economically as well as politically backward situation when compared with other European countries. "Voltaire had declared that Germany was condemned to eternal poverty" [Henderson, 1959, p. 2]. Trade was hampered by insufficient transport facilities, by "a grotesque system of duties and dues" [Dawson, 1904, p. 8] in each state. Some 1800 customs frontiers existed in Germany in 1790 [ibid., p. 21] and the situation was improved only slightly by the territorial consolidations of Napoleon. In several states imports of many commodities were prohibited, which resulted in large scale smuggling. Not even state revenues, largely tariff revenues, could be raised efficiently by such a trading system. As King Frederick William III of Prussia noted: "I am shocked at the voluminous excise and customs tariffs" [Dawson, 1904, p. 9].

115. The hopes for economic and political reforms inside the Germanic Confederation were disappointed because of the divergent interests and economic conditions of the member states. Yet, parallel to the unsuccessful attempts of liberals in the "Bundestag" (Federal Diet), the Prussian bureaucracy under the intellectual leadership of Stein and Hardenberg prepared "the reorganization of the State" as Hardenberg wrote in his Memorandum of September, 1807. The proposed program aimed at giving Prussia the greatest possible amount of freedom - in thought, in speech, in action, in trade, in industry, in government [Dawson, 1904]. In this overall program of political and economic liberalization trade policy was just one element, albeit an important one. Stein's "Instruction to the Royal Governments of the Prussian Provinces", dealing with trade policy, shows deep economic insight: "Together with this liberty, facility of communication and freedom of trade both at home and abroad are also necessary if our industry, trade, and welfare are to thrive. Thus those industries will naturally come into being which can be carried on to the best advantage, and which are the most suited to the economic condition of the country and the civilization of the nation. It is a mistake to believe that it is advantageous to a State to produce itself articles which can be bought more cheaply abroad. The increased costs of production caused by manufacturing them are an absolute loss, and had they been employed in another industry would have given abundant gain. It is a distorted view that one should in such a case seek to keep the money in the country, and rather not buy at all. ... It is not necessary to favor trade; it must simply not be obstructed. Freedom of trade and of industry creates the greatest possible competition between the producing and consuming public, and protects the consumers most effectively against scarcity and excessive prices" [cited in Dawson, 1904, p. 11].

116. When in May 1818, the new Prussian tariff law was promulgated, tariff rates were just one part of the reform. Most importantly, it "abolished the ancient Akzise in favor of a border tax on trade and so ended the collection of duties at the town gate; it eliminated the legal distinction between town and country side and provided for free movements of goods between them as well as of occupations." [Dumke, 1977, p. 248]. Thus it created for the first time a national free trade area within Prussia. It is likely that the positive economic effects of the tariff law

were at first gains from an internal free market and a lower administrative burden. The tariff was a specific tariff designed mainly under two premises:

- It should provide sufficient funds to the government while, at the same time, it should not injure Prussian business interests.

- Moderate effective protection was desired for manufacturing - the infant industry argument was already known.

117. These goals were thought to be met by a tariff structure of zero tariffs for raw materials, a 20-30 percent ad valorem equivalent tariff on "Kolonialwaren" (tropical and subtropical products), and about a 10 percent tariff on other commodities [Henderson, 1959, p. 40]. Free traders in other countries consequently praised the Prussian tariff law. Huskisson said in the House of Commons: "I trust that the time will come when we can say as much for the tariff of this country" [Henderson, 1959, p. 43]. It was generally regarded as the lowest tariff in Europe [Kindleberger, 1978, p. 56]. However, falling world market prices in the 1820's led to considerable increases in ad valorem equivalent duties. Rough estimates for selected goods reveal large variations in duties with a level well over 10 percent. Rates over 80 percent for manufactures are reported [Henderson, 1959, p. 4]. Ohnishi [1973] calculated ad valorem equivalent duties of 9-35 percent for fine cotton goods, 9-84.3 percent for woollens, and 15.6-91.6 percent for rough iron goods [Dumke, 1977, Table II, p. 93].

118. In interpreting the Prussian reforms, one should distinguish between the intention and the outcome of policy. Intentions were probably focussed more on internal liberalization and administrative reform. The reform led to a liberal trade policy in addition to a common market and fiscal unity inside Prussia. Free internal markets without the Akzise made it necessary to design an external tariff. Tariff policy, in turn was dominated by revenue considerations. But since the previous system consisted of prohibitions and immensely inefficient duties, a move toward a rational tariff with moderate effective protection for manufactures and high revenues resulted in a low average nominal tariff when compared to the rest of the world.

119. There are many reasons why Prussia was among the first countries to design a new tariff after the Napoleonic Wars. As already mentioned, the new tariff was just a part of several economic reforms which themselves were determined not only be economic considerations. The political and ideological climate surely contributed to its success. The ideologically moving force was the Prussian bureaucracy which, after becoming exposed to the writings of Adam Smith, favored market oriented solutions to overcome economic backwardness. Kindleberger [1978, p. 190] reports that a "provincial leader wrote in 1796 that he made it a practice to start each day by reading a passage from The Wealth of Nations". Aided by the Prussian hierarchical structure and a lack of alternative proposals these ideas were soon adopted by the rulers.

120. The ensuing years give evidence of the remarkable success of the Prussian reforms. True, internal economic growth was moderate at best, yet this was mostly due to a lack of capital, communications, and technology - factors which develop with a considerable time lag only. The government's budget situation, however, improved noticeably, to a large extent due to higher than expected tariff revenues [Ohnishi, 1973, p. 122 ff.]. With these funds, increased investment in infrastructure became feasible, and Prussia's foreign influence improved parallel to her financial situation. Numerous treaties with neighboring states and enclaves resulted in the geographic expansion of the Prussian customs system.

121. There were several reasons for these states to enter into such agreements:

- smuggling, a substitute for legal trade, became more difficult with the new tariff borders;

- the internal liberalization in Prussia seemed to work like a customs union, leading to internal trade creation and external trade diversion such that, despite relatively low tariff barriers, market entry became more difficult;

- falling world market prices led to rising ad valorem tariffs - an effect the Prussian government did not compensate.

Those states that did not come to an agreement with Prussia attempted to initiate internal economic reforms by themselves and to form customs unions with others. By 1828 three customs unions existed in Germany: the Prussian-Hessian Customs Union dominated by Prussia; the South German Union; and the Central German Union consisting of small states mainly in central Germany. The latter's common objective hardly amounted to more than keeping roads open and preventing the two other unions from expanding.

3. The Zollverein (The German Customs Union)

122. When in January 1834 the treaty of the Deutsche Zollverein came into effect almost twenty years had passed since the first proposal for giving customs authority to the Germanic Confederation in 1815. It then took until 1885 for Germany to complete the common political and customs frontier; in this year the City of Bremen joined the customs system of the German Empire. Figure 1 shows the evolution of the German external tariff from 1834. The whole period was characterized by intense negotiations in the Germanic Confederation and by opposition of Germany's neighbors to the formation of the Zollverein. Fischer [1972, p. 128] characterizes the Zollverein as an "example of political circumspection in a world of emergencies demanding relief". Considering the advantages of a customs union it is surprising why it took so long to reach the agreement of 1834. The economic benefits to the member states of the Zollverein were so large that one must attribute the 15 years of negotiation more to conflicting political interests and tactical maneuvering than to the difficulty of achieving an economically-acceptable compromise. From the formation of the Zollverein two main effects can be isolated: It dramatically increased state revenues and it led to some internal trade creation.

123. Internal trade creation was induced by the changes in internal and external trade barriers. The common uniform external tariff - basically the Prussian tariff of 1818 - was the highest in any German state so far. Internally, free trade prevailed with few exceptions. Compared to the

Figure 1 - Average Duties Paid in Germany, 1830-1984

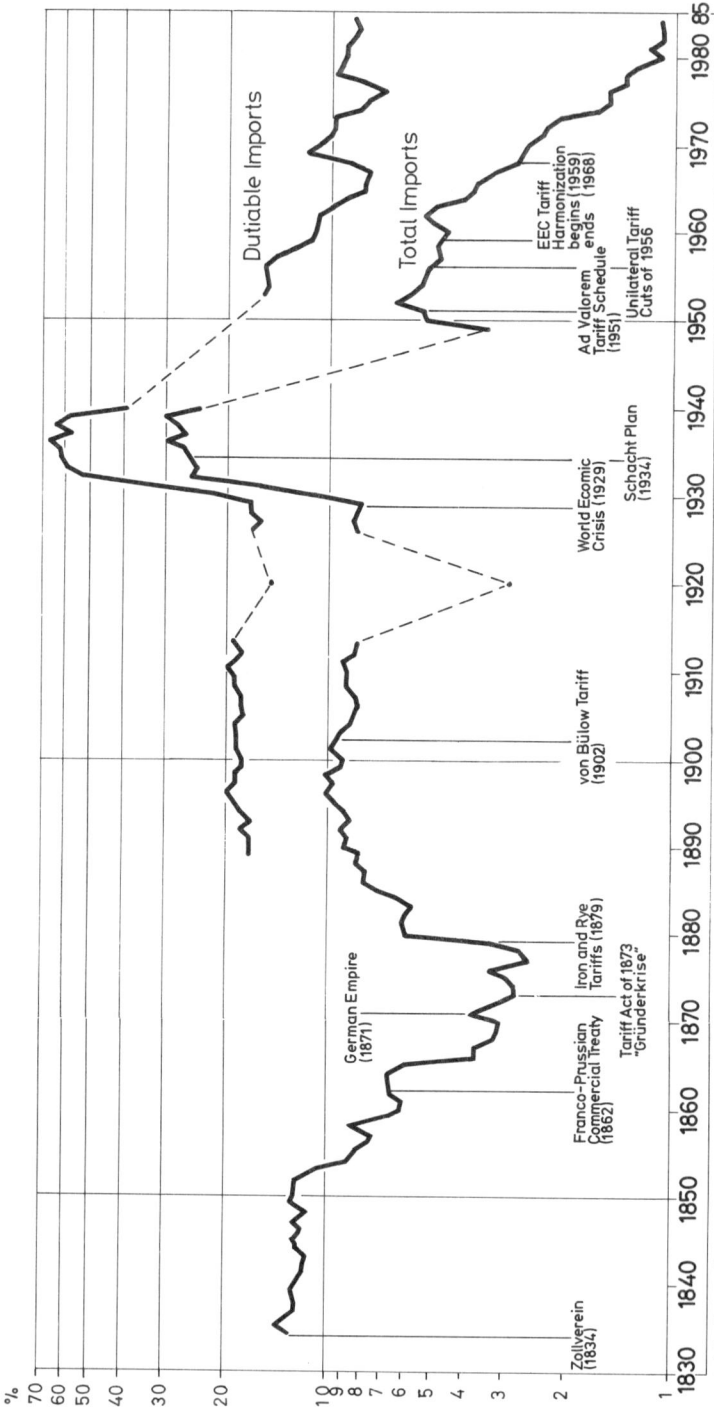

(a) Duties collected as a per cent of imports. - (b) Specific duties until 1951.

Source: Borries [1970]; Kaiserliches Statistisches Amt [various issues]; Statistisches Reichsamt [various issues]; Statistisches Bundesamt [h; i].

1800 customs frontiers existing in 1790 [Henderson, 1959] this change should have large welfare effects. Because of the large number of states an empirical assessment of static and dynamic welfare gains is difficult. Dumke [1977] estimated an increase in real income of about 1.5 percent for the southern German states. This rather low gain is not surprising if one considers that only 16.6 percent of total Zollverein trade was intra-trade and that the south's extra Zollverein imports comprise 80 percent of its total imports [ibid., p. 315-317].

124. Economies of scale, accelerated diffusion of technology, greater competition, and risk reduction are all factors which are generally considered to accompany the formation of a customs union. Without wishing to stress causal relations too far, the period of the Zollverein can be characterized as a time of large-scale investments in infrastructure and human capital - made possible, e.g., by increased state revenues. Technical universities were established in Karlsruhe (1825), Darmstadt (1826), Munich (1827), and so on. Also extensive visits of specialists to Great Britain were initiated to facilitate technology transfer. The introduction of railways and an extensive road building program accompanied trade liberalization. For some smaller states the threat of locating roads around their territory induced their first steps in entering larger customs areas [Henderson, 1959, p. 75 f.]. Although one cannot assess these dynamic effects quantitatively, their combined impact surely led to more competition and better allocation of resources.

125. The most important effect of the Zollverein, however, was the increase in net state revenues. This came about through a combination of reducing transaction costs and reducing smuggling by a cheaper policing of the Zollverein borders more carefully. Prussian civil servants, such as Ludwig Kuehne, director general of taxation in Prussia from 1842-1849, were well aware of this relationship [Dumke, 1976, p. 41 f.]. Kuehne's prediction for the savings in administration cost came very close to those actually realized. The Zollverein resulted in the elimination of 781.5 "Meilen" of customs borders. Given estimated administration cost of 2000 taler per "Meile" of border, Dumke [1976, p. 43] estimated a yearly saving of 1.56 million taler per year, equivalent to just under one percent of Zollverein National Income.

84

126. Not only reductions in administration costs due to shorter custom borders are important for tariff revenues. The net gain also depends on the geographic size of a state. Since higher tariffs induce more smuggling, which in turn requires higher enforcement expenditure, net revenues and protection cannot be increased just by raising tariffs. On the contrary, Dumke [1976, p. 45] found that only 10 out of the 35 independent states in Germany were able to maintain a tariff system that yielded positive net revenues. Of those, only two - Bavaria and Prussia - were able to provide protection and revenues at the same time (1). The other states had no customs system at all or relied on a variety of relatively low charges. It is apparent that especially the smaller states gained from joining the Zollverein in two ways: they increased their revenues and their protection against non-Zollverein states. This revenue increase brought, according to Dumke [1976, p. 46 f.], another 2.95 million taler per year from 1835 onwards to the Zollverein treasury. "This is 24 percent of the average net customs revenue of the Zollverein of the years 1834 to 1845" [ibid., p. 47]. The importance of revenue considerations is further illuminated by comparing the total tariff revenue gain of 4.51 million taler per year to the total real income increase of 6.74 million taler per year in South Germany attributable to trade creation.

127. These financial aspects constituted overwhelming incentives for smaller states to join the Zollverein. For the first time many were able to obtain tariff revenues at all. This fact was also important in the political considerations of the monarchs of these states. On the one hand they undoubtedly lost sovereignty to the Zollverein, i.e. to Prussia as the hegemonic power. On the other hand, tariff revenues collected by the Zollverein gave them more internal freedom, as a British source stated in 1835: "[The Zollverein] assured to the princes their revenue without the trouble of collecting, and without the inconvenience of applying to turbulent chambers for their supplies. It might be thought that the

---

(1) But even Bavaria had a disadvantage compared to Prussia. The South German Customs Union only had per capita customs revenues of 9.5 silver groschen compared to 24 in Prussia. Also administration costs amounted to 44 percent of gross revenue, whereas Prussia lost only 15-20 percent [Henderson, 1959, p. 63].

chambers would have resisted to the death this fatal blow at their national independence; but no! the members were landed proprietors, or manufacturers; to the first was pointed out that the taxes were now to be be taken off the land, and laid upon commerce; to the second, that domestic, that national, that their produce was to take the place of foreign manufacturers" [cited in Dumke, 1976, p. 57].

Purely economic factors as well as political economy therefore point to the princes of the smaller states favoring the Zollverein. Henderson [1958, p. 95] summarizes the attitude of the majority of states: "The states concerned fought for their own narrow interests and many of them joined the Zollverein only when economic depression and empty exchequers made further resistance to Prussia impossible".

128. Whereas state finances were the decisive argument for joining the Zollverein for small states not able to administer a profitable tariff system, for the larger states, especially Württemberg and Bavaria, financial pressures were less important. They could afford to foster their political independence. Only a common enemy, the Central German Customs Union, finally brought the Prussian-Hessian Customs Union together with the South German Customs Union [Fischer, 1972, p. 113]. But Bavaria and Württemberg still retained the right to negotiate commercial treaties with foreign countries after joining the Zollverein [Henderson, 1959, p. 93].

129. The historical studies of the pre-Zollverein era and the economic consequences of the Zollverein lead one to conclude that the advantages of a customs union with more than marginal economic benefits to all participants cannot account for the lengthy and hard negotiations before the Zollverein materialized. Rather, political considerations in the German states slowed down a process whose economic dynamism could hardly be stopped. With Prussia negotiating commercial treaties in the name of the Zollverein, these states could not be sure that Prussia would act in the interest of the Zollverein. In addition, the threat-potential of Prussia was immense. A collapse of the Zollverein would completely strip the small states of their tariff revenues. The southern states also would experience severe losses, since they had increased the share of tariffs in

net state revenues from about 7 percent to about 15 percent (1819-1849), [Dumke, 1972, p. 96]. Prussia, on the other hand, had only an increase from 14.5 percent to 17.3 percent over the same period [ibid.]. Financial prosperity of the state treasures and economic prosperity of business were therefore paid for by giving hegemonical power to Prussia.

130. The years of the Zollverein from 1834 to national unification in 1871 were governed by this relationship. Several crises ended in a deadlock, leaving the Zollverein essentially unchanged. With the political power of Prussia growing, the conflict with Austria was inevitable and became one of the decisive factors of Prussian politics in the 1860's. The natural enlargement of the Zollverein would have been the inclusion of Austria. The Austrian Minister of Commerce (1848-1851) and Finance (1855-1860) Freiherr von Bruck made several unsuccessful attempts in this direction (1). The only positive result was the Austro-Prussian treaty of 1853, where Prussia - in the name of the Zollverein - and Austria granted each other Most-Favored-Nation (MFN) treatment [Henderson, 1959, p. 223]. The political rivalry between these two states also became an important factor in Germany's move towards free trade from 1860 onwards.

4. The Rise and Fall of Free Trade

a. The Move towards Free Trade

131. All over Europe, the 1860's mark the breakthrough towards free trade. It started in Great Britain and - by a coincidence of favorable factors - spread to France and its neighbors. This historically remarkable process was facilitated by prosperity in Europe. The increasing spread of industrialization on the continent promoted trade relations and free trade sentiment at the same time. In this climate, national trade

---

(1) See Henderson [1959] and Böhme [1966] for a historical survey.

policies underwent considerable change, reflecting evolving internal political structures.

132. The revolution of 1848 already marked a change in the political climate. Liberal ideas and nationalism were introduced with increasing force in public as well as in parliament. In 1858 the "Kongress Deutscher Volkswirte" (Congress of German Economists) was founded. It was a national organization which brought together intellectuals and businessmen in their endeavor to achieve freedom of trade and freedom of movement [Erdmann, 1968, p. 242]. Many of its members in turn were members of various parliaments, influential leaders in political parties and associations. Their combined influence inside and outside the parliaments induced a change in public opinion towards liberalization in internal economic policy as well as in trade policy. Opposing groups such as the "Industrie-Börsenverein" (founded in 1859) were not nationally organized. The "Industrie-Börsenverein" was a loose association of south German cotton industrialists allegedly founded as a reaction to the establishment of the Kongress Deutscher Volkswirte [Erdmann, 1968, p. 207]. Regional orientation was its main handicap, since it had no backing from the powerful Prussian politicians. In this situation the lack of political unification in Germany prevented other protectionist groups from organizing a successful opposition against the free traders.

133. This free-trade-oriented internal climate was accompanied by the continuing struggle for German political unity, either as the "Small German" solution excluding Austria or the "Great German" solution including Austria. In this political struggle, Prussia and Austria competed for hegemony in Germany. Trade policy, and in particular the Franco-Prussian Commercial Treaty, became objects of this dispute (1). Bismarck, for whom trade policy was always subordinated to power politics, had several reasons to promote free trade in the 1850's and 1860's. The majority in the Federal Diet was pro-free trade as were the influential Prussian Junkers, the rural aristocracy. At the same time high-tariff Austria was still negotiating her membership in the Zollverein.

----

(1) A detailed and careful account of this struggle can be found in Böhme [1966]. The present summary draws on this book.

Yet, Austrian industrialists successfully blocked any tariff concessions proposed by Bruck. A free trade position by Bismarck therefore undermined attempts by the southern states to balance Prussia's hegemonic position with Austrian membership.

134. When the Franco-Prussian Commercial Treaty was initialled in March 1862 (see Figure 1) it was clear that - in the case of agreement by the rest of the member states of the Zollverein - there was no chance for Austria joining the Zollverein in the foreseeable future. In the ensuing negotiations between Prussia and the Zollverein states in 1865, Bismarck even threatened to let Prussia's membership lapse in case the treaty was not signed by the Zollverein. In addition, in this treaty Prussia granted MFN treatment to France, thus violating the 1853 treaty between Austria and the Zollverein in which the signatories granted each other preferential treatment. The political struggle finally ended with the renewal of the Zollverein in October 1865 on the basis of the Franco-Prussian Treaty of 1862.

135. Purely economic considerations, of course, were present in the Prussian and Zollverein decision to liberalize its tariff. Treaties similar to the Cobden-Chevalier Treaty were signed by France with Belgium (1861), Italy (1863), Switzerland (1864), Sweden, Norway, the Hanseatic Cities, Spain and Holland in 1865. These treaties threatened the competitive position of German producers in those markets and led to more pressure for trade liberalization in the Zollverein. These economic and political changes led to the reorientation of the Zollverein's trade policy. In addition to the Franco-Prussian Treaty similar commercial treaties were signed by Prussia in 1865 with Great Britain, Belgium and Italy [Henderson, 1959, p. 273]. Transport on rivers and at sea also became liberalized. Together with the removal or mitigation of transition duties, the foundation for a strong expansion in foreign trade was set.

136. In 1867 the "Zollparlament" (Customs Parliament) and the "Zollbundesrat" (Customs Council) were established. In this reform unanimous decisions were not required anymore, thus making trade policy more flexible. Free-trade sentiment grew among the public and increasingly influenced the members of these bodies. A tariff bill brought before the

Zollparlament by the Zollbundesrat had to be withdrawn several times upon the reproach of not being liberal enough. After several revisions, the new tariff bill, a compromise between extreme free traders - the northern Hanseatic Cities, the "Handelstag", the Prussian agrarians, and so on - and moderate protectionists - mainly special interest groups such as the "Verein der Zollvereinsländischen Eisenhütten" (Union of Ironworks of the Zollverein) as well as some southern states - passed the Zollparlament on May 7, 1870 [Lambi, 1963, ch. 4].

137. This action by the Zollparlament was not yet the final step towards free trade. Although grain had been duty free since 1865, even in the 1870 tariff bill. pig iron and rough iron and textiles still had considerable protection, of which the former was strongly opposed by the agrarians. These questions were overshadowed by the Franco-Prussian war of 1870/71 and the founding of the German Empire. But in 1872 the free traders continued to press for the abandoning of all tariffs. Their case was eased because revenue considerations became less pressing as French reparation payments were received. Only a few iron industrialists opposed the abolition of iron duties. In 1873 the new tariff passed the Reichstag with a repeal of duties on pig iron (see Figure 1). Iron goods, nets for fishing and soda were to become duty free on January 1, 1877 [Zimmermann, 1901, p. 228].

This final triumph of the free-trade movement already showed that the peak was past. The political climate was changing. Germany's free-trade policy in the late 1860's and early 1870's had not been honored by reciprocal tariff concessions from other countries, the economic crisis of the mid-1870's was already expected. Most important, however, the defeat on the 1870 tariff bill convinced protectionists that they needed a national coordination of their interests just like the free traders had in the "Handelstag" and the "Kongress der Volkswirte".

b. The Rise of Nationwide Interest Groups

138. The 1873 decision to postpone repeal of the iron tariffs until 1877 was considered a defeat by free traders. And rightly so, the "Verein

Deutscher Eisengießereien" (Union of German Iron Foundries) which had fought against free trade before 1873 and the "Verein zur Wahrung der gemeinsamen wirtschaftlichen Interessen in Rheinland-Westfalen" (Union for the Promotion of the Common Economic Interests of Rhineland-Westphalia) or "Langnamverein" (1) which was founded by the former union, were convinced that for successful agitation their interests must be represented on a broader basis. In November 1873, a number of Westphalian iron masters formed the "Verein Deutscher Eisen- und Stahl-Industrieller" (Union of the German Iron and Steel Manufacturers), the first nationwide protectionist lobby.

139. Meanwhile the boom after the Franco-Prussian War of 1870/71 came to an end in 1873. It had started with a rapid monetary expansion due to French reparations, which were paid faster than expected. The increased financial resources of the government were used for infrastructure and military consumption. The rapid expansion is illustrated by the increase in the production of the iron and steel industry; its output increased from 1527 thousand tons in 1870 to 2440 thousand tons in 1873 – a quantity not reached again until 1878 [Kaiserliches Statistisches Amt, 1882, p. 33]. The turning point was the Vienna stock market crisis in 1873, which soon spread to stock markets all over the world. It was followed by a worldwide recession and falling prices. "On all iron products other than agricultural machinery the prices of 1878 were 50-60 percent below those of 1873" [Lambi, 1963, p. 76].

140. This course of events undoubtedly helped the iron and steel industry in their agitation by attributing the recession to the free trade decision in 1873, a political trick described by Corden [1987] as "guilt by association". Yet, their first attempts to infiltrate the free trade organizations such as the "Kongress Deutscher Volkswirte" and the "Verein für Socialpolitik" failed [Lambi, 1963, Ch. VII; Böhme, 1966, p. 359 ff.]. In 1875 a repeal of the iron tariffs was defeated as well [Böhme, 1966, p. 377 ff.]. One of the major obstacles to successful agitation of the protectionist lobbies was their lack of unity. Each interest group propagated its own narrow interests, in many cases neutralizing

---

(1) Bismarck called it this because of its long name: "lang[er] Nam[e]".

each other. Leading members of the "Langnamverein" therefore tried to broaden the base of the protectionist movement [see Lambi, 1963, Ch. VIII]. The widening economic crisis meanwhile had affected the traditionally protectionist southern textile industry as well as other industries. When in 1876 the "Centralverband Deutscher Industrieller (CDI)" (Central Association of German Industrialists) was founded it was dominated by the "Langnamverein" and the "Verein Süddeutscher Baumwollindustrieller" (Union of South German Cotton Industrialists). The "Verein Deutscher Eisen- und Stahlindustrieller" joined in 1877. In the following years the CDI expanded to become the dominating interest group of German industry. It included neither agriculture nor commerce.

141. A second attempt to pass protectionist legislation in the Reichstag in 1877 was rejected by the coalition of agrarians, commercial and political laissez-faire liberals [Lambi, 1963, p. 130]. It became clear that without some sort of agreement with agrarian interests the free trade majority in the Reichstag and in the bureaucracy could not be defeated. The political power structure in the Reich gave overwhelming influence to Prussian politicians in the parliament as well as in the bureaucracy [Fischer, 1972, p. 202](1). In Prussia a semi-governmental agricultural organization, the "Landesökonomiekollegium", had already existed since 1842 [Fischer, 1972, p. 196]. The representatives (Landesökonomieräte) fulfilled both governmental duties and agitated for the interests of agriculture. Dominated by the Junkers, their activities were all free-trade oriented since this group accounted for the majority of grain exports. External shocks to German and especially Prussian agriculture helped to turn their stand on trade policy matters.

142. The signs observed in Germany were falling grain prices and a deterioration of the trade balance in grain, and later in temperate zone foodstuffs in general. Rye prices fell most, from 175 marks/ton in 1873 to 132 marks/ton in 1878. In particular, Prussian farmers were adversely affected by the drop in rye prices, since they were growing rye on about one third of their cultivated land [Statistisches Reichsamt, 1881, p. 25]. The underlying reasons for this development were first of all the

---

(1) Eschenburg [1955], however, questions such influence.

92

rapid expansion of agricultural output in the United States, and secondly, the loss of the natural protection of high transport cost. For example, US wheat production almost doubled between 1870 and 1879, while
exports almost tripled [Lambi, 1963, p. 132]. In 1878 US wheat exports
of 4 096 678 tons [ibid.] compared to a total wheat production in Germany of 2 278 696 tons [Statistisches Reichsamt, 1881, p. 24]. The
North American railroads made the export of Midwestern grain to Europe
profitable. These developments did not so much lead to increased German
imports of American grain as to diminishing market shares on the British
market. By 1879, the United States and Canada supplied 68.2 percent of
British grain imports, while Germany's share had fallen to 2.9 percent
[Lambi, 1965, p. 133].

143. The bad harvest of 1876 illustrated another effect of a free trade
policy on agricultural incomes. Under autarky small harvests go hand in
hand with higher prices, thus stabilizing agricultural incomes. World
market prices, however, are determined almost independently of such
regional variability in yields. In all cases of domestic supply fluctua-
tions, incomes fluctuate more under such a regime. Therefore the experience of 1876 made the farmers who were oriented towards local markets more inclined to switch to a protectionist policy than the export
oriented large estates in the east. The first agricultural association that
joined the demands of the iron and steel industry was the "Volkswirt-
schaftlicher Verein für das Rheinland" (Economic Union for the Rhine-
land). Not only its proximity to the industrial center but also the easy
transport channels for American grain explain this change in policies.

The export-oriented estates in the east, organized in the "Vereinigung
der Steuer- und Wirtschaftsreformer" (Association for the Reform of
Taxation and the Economy) of 1876, turned protectionist only slowly. To
this group the first goal was a reorientation of taxation away from fixed
capital to other sources. Increased tariff revenues seemed a worthwhile
alternative for raising government revenues [Zimmermann, 1901, p. 273].

144. Even though there was no unanimous support for protection policies
in their respective clientele the agrarian as well as industrial organizations became increasingly dominated by protectionists. The general

agreement on both sides to favor a reinstatement of tariffs for iron as well as for grain was however contrasted by the inability of both groups to settle on the proposed tariff structure. The protectionist sentiment was still contrasted by the economic insight that each group should support free trade for the others and protection for their own commodities. The final return to a protectionist trade policy, then, was merely prepared by the lobbies. They did not get beyond protectionist propaganda until 1879. It was, again, changing interests in foreign policy which made it feasible to write and pass the tariff reform law in 1879.

c. The Return to Protection

145. The founding of national interest groups in Germany changed the political climate. In the late 1860's and early 1870's public opinion was dominated by the free-trade agitation of the liberal associations; after 1876 protectionists first gained influence in their respective industrial organizations such as the CDI and in the agrarian unions. Free trade oriented industries and farmers were outvoiced in public debate. This process then carried over to political parties and elections. In 1878 protectionists for the first time had a majority of votes in the Reichstag.

146. Nevertheless, the "iron and rye" coalition of the CDI and the Junker-dominated "Vereinigung der Steuer- und Wirtschaftsreformer" could not agree on a compromise for the proposal of a new tariff, despite their common interest in passing such a legislation. Again it was Bismarck who saw a coincidence between protectionist interests and his own. He was not interested in the welfare aspects of alternative trade policy frameworks as becomes evident from his writings [see, e.g., Lambi, 1963, Ch. XI; Dawson, 1904, Chs. IV, V]. Trade policy Bismarck regarded as "a part of internal policy of the German Empire, connecting it to the problem of Imperial strength and unity, the issue of taxation, the relationship between the executive and the legislative powers, and the balance of political parties in the Reichstag" as it is characterized by Lambi [1963, p. 163].

147. Protectionist interests of "iron and rye" coincided with Bismarck's interest in revenues which the Reich could raise without depending on the Bundestag and the states. In favoring a more or less uniform tariff, he hoped for consensus among the diverging interests of industries and agriculture. In several other political decisions collaboration with the protectionist majority also seemed more advantageous to him. Just as he had backed free traders in the Zollverein to further his political interests for the Small-German solution twenty years earlier, he switched to protectionist policies. In his mercantilist attitude he supported high tariffs as a bargaining chip for trade negotiations with France, Austria, and Russia.

148. Each actor in this situation had different objectives in mind, but all were united by the belief that increased tariffs would achieve their goals. In July 1879, the "almost" free-trade era of Germany came to an end. Grain and iron tariffs were reintroduced and other tariffs raised (see Figure 1). Ad valorem rates were approximately at their 1868 levels with industrial products facing a 10-15 percent tariff [Lambi, 1963, p. 226]. The average tariff doubled from somewhat below 3 percent to about 6 percent (see Figure 1). According to the estimates of effective rates of protection by Webb [1977], the winner was the cartellized iron industry with 12 percent, followed by rye and wheat with 9 percent, whereas hogs had a negative effective rate of protection of -1 percent.

149. The tariff of 1879 was considered a success of the CDI [Böhme, 1966, p. 562]. The tariff on wheat of 10 marks per ton amounted to only a 5 percent ad valorem rate whereas raw iron was protected by an approximately 15 percent ad valorem rate [Fremdling, 1987, p. 36]. This unsatisfactory situation for the agrarian interests was changed in the following years. Due to increasing influence of the East-Elbian aristocracy in the "Vereinigung der Steuer- und Wirtschaftsreformer" [Böhme, 1966, p. 401 f.] and in the parliament [Gerschenkron, 1943, p. 148] grain tariffs rose to 30 marks in 1885 and 50 marks per ton in 1887. Effective rates of protection in 1889/90 went up to 48 percent (rye) and 35 percent (wheat), whereas those for iron remained constant [Webb, 1977, pp. 349 and 355].

150. In the last quarter of the 19th century, the German economy underwent rapid structural changes which was only partly reflected in the development of interest groups and their internal and external policies. One would expect increasing influence of more innovative, modern industries in the CDI. In the agrarian groups farmers producing foodstuffs for local markets, such as vegetables and dairy products, also should have become more influential. Both of these groups favor low prices on their inputs, i.e. on grain. Therefore their interests should be directly opposed to the "iron and rye" coalition of CDI and the "Verein der Wirtschafts- und Steuerreformer".

Yet, the reaction in industry differed from that in agriculture. The growing dissatisfaction of the export oriented light industry led to a split up of the CDI. With the encouragement of the "Chemieverein" (Chemicals Union) which in 1889 had already left the CDI, the "Bund der Industriellen" (BdI, Union of Industrialists) was founded in 1895. It united small and medium size firms and was organized under the principle of one vote for each member combined with low membership fees (1). Without contacts to the administration and working with little resources, the BdI gained little influence [Blaich, 1979, p. 35 ff.]. Chances for coalitions in trade policy questions were slim mainly for political reasons. In the Reichstag only the SPD and left-wing liberals were still supporting free trade policies and these groups had no other common political ground on which to cooperate with the BdI.

151. The Junkers, on the other hand, boosted their dominating role as representatives of agriculture without loosing the support of the small farmers. After having complete control over the "Verein der Wirtschafts- und Steuerreformer", they founded the Bund der Landwirte (BdL - Agrarian League) in 1893. It was a reaction to the slight lowering of grain tariffs in bilateral treaties with Austria, Russia, and others which Leo von Caprivi, the Imperial Chancellor, had concluded in 1891. In

(1) The BdI had a membership fee of 5 marks per year. The CDI minimum fee was 100 marks. With higher payments, however, a member could buy more votes. Specifically, 100-299 marks admitted one delegate, 300-599 marks admitted two delegates, and for each additional 300 marks one extra delegate was allowed.

order to mediate the opposition of the Junkers, Caprivi abolished the certification of origin which was needed to get a tariff refund for reexported grain. This amounted to a considerable export subsidy to the Junkers. Yet, they further increased their demands. In the "Antrag Kanitz" (Kanitz motion), as it has become known, they asked for a state grain-import monopoly which should fix grain prices at the average of the 1850-1890 prices. As a consequence German grain prices would have been about 100 percent above world market prices [Gerschenkron, 1943, p. 53]. Although the bill was repeatedly defeated in the Reichstag, it was introduced again and again.

152. These events shed an interesting light on the form in which trade policy disputes were conducted in Germany at the end of the 19th century. The agitation against free trade more and more turned into an amalgam of political ideology and demagoguery. Antisemitism went hand in hand with opposition to stock markets, futures markets, and industrialization in general. Overall, one can conclude that the Junkers succeeded in turning the trade policy debate which was discussed as an economic question into a political debate on nationalism and on the preservation of the old society [Barkin, 1970, Ch. 4]. Reichskanzler von Bülow, for exemple, told Emperor Wilhelm II: "I hold increased protection for agriculture absolutely necessary out of economic, and still more out of social, political, and national grounds ... The cities are swelling into a hypertrophied state, the land is being depopulated. Therein lies the great danger, not only from the standpoint of our military strength, for the land delivers, all in all, better soldiers than the cities, but for our whole social structure" [cited in Barkin, 1970, p. 220].

153. The coalition between the Junker-dominated BdL and the iron-industry dominated CDI on trade policy against free traders in the "Deutsche Handelstag" (DHT, German Trade Council) and the BdI entailed a mixture of economic and political compromises. Contemporary writers such as Naumann emphasized the power politics of the tariff policy debate: "All economic debate is only the accompaniment of a bitter struggle for power in the state. The present leaders of the tariff movement were themselves free traders thirty years ago. At that time free trade was the path to power ... The tariff is not to be conceived of as an economic

measure; as such it is and must remain incomprehensible. It is a foray
of political will into the economy. As an old, tested ruling class, the
grain nobility knows the limits of its power, and would rather share it
with the iron barons than give it up" [cited in Barkin, 1970, p. 202].

It also was a compromise between economic interests. The agrarians used
their opposition against the "Mittellandkanal" (1) and the naval program
as a bargaining chip. The CDI proposed backing the BdL in its demand
for higher tariffs in return for agrarian support for the state investment
programs noted [Blaich, 1979, p. 27 ff.].

The "von Bülow" tariff of 1902 (see Figure 1) then incorporated increased protection for grain from 25-30 percent to 40-50 percent
[Fremdling, 1986, p. 37]. The decrease in comparative advantage of
grain growing in East Germany was mitigated but not solved. Even
though the Junkers' economic influence was deteriorating, they established their political power. Similarly, the large-scale iron and steel industry benefited from the demand boost of the naval and canal projects.

5. The Interwar Period

154. In the Treaty of Versailles (Art. 268) Germany had to grant MFN
treatment to all signatories of the treaty for five years. Tariff rates
were fixed at their 1914 levels for six months, except for grain and vegetables, whose tariff rates were fixed for three years. Under the treaty,
the practical prohibition of foreign trade which had been introduced in
1917 ("Verordnung über die Regelung der Einfuhr, vom 16. Januar
1917") for imports, and during 1914/15 for exports, was repealed. The
more important decision, however, concerns what later became the famous
"Loch im Westen" (hole in the West). In the occupied territories west of
the Rhine, German tariff laws were not enacted. This hole - it was believed - made Germany practically a free trade area [Haberland, 1927,

(1) It was to connect the Rhine with the Elbe and thus allow shipping
    from the Atlantic into eastern Germany.

p. 38 ff.]. Therefore, wartime administrative controls were reinstituted at all Rhine crossings. In 1920 the import controls were extended to almost goods entering Germany. Very little statistical information on Germany exists for the period 1914-1925. From the sketchy information available one can conclude that foodstuffs, especially grain imports were allowed [Röpke, 1934, p. 56]. But devaluation together with internal price controls led to a grain price level below world market prices [Gerschenkron, 1943, p. 107], and hence, pressure to export, not import.

155. The German Government reacted to the beginning of the hyperinflation and the devaluation of the Reichsmark with export controls in the same way as they had been used during World War I. Export duties were introduced because it was feared that the devaluation of the Reichsmark would lead to the "Ausverkauf Deutschlands" (sellout of Germany) [Haberland, 1927, p. 51]. These tight controls and interventions remained in place until 1924, when hyperinflation was stopped and a return to a normal trade policy seemed appropriate to political decision makers.

156. In the meantime, a general trend towards more protectionist trade policies in most countries became evident. As a consequence of World War I many industries had been built which - under peacetime prices - turned out to be uncompetitive. Naturally, the demand for protection from such industries increased. Already in 1920 Great Britain had imposed the "Dyestuffs Act" directed mostly against German exports. Other industries were protected by over 30 percent tariffs in the "Safeguarding of Industries Act" in 1921 and 1925 [Blaich, 1985, p. 29]. The United States, through the Fordney-McCumber Tariff in 1922 imposed tariff barriers of 50 to 80 percent, in some cases of up to 200 percent These were raised even further in the Smoot-Hawley Act of 1930 [Blaich, 1985, p. 30].

157. Already in 1921 the "Reichswirtschaftsministerium" (Imperial Ministry of the Economy) had started to design a tariff which was to replace the Bülow tariff of 1902 by 1925. The "Reichsverband der Deutschen In-

dustrie" (RDI) (1) established a trade policy commission which was influential in the design of the tariff reform. Still, the old conflicts between the export-oriented modern industry and the protectionist basic industries remained. In 1924 inside the RDI the "Arbeitsgemeinschaft der Eisenverarbeitenden Industrie" (AVI-Working group of the metal working industries) was formed with the intention of counterbalancing the influence of the revised solidarity bloc of 1902 between agriculture and heavy industry. In the presence of rising trade barriers imposed by most of Germany's trading partners and under the pressure of protectionist groups, the AVI settlement of 1925 ended in a protectionist compromise with special treatment for AVI members. They were reimbursed the difference between world market and domestic price for any raw materials or half-finished products which were imported for the production of export goods [Blaich, 1979, p. 76].

158. The tariff reform of 1925 raised tariffs considerably over their 1913 levels for textiles, automobiles, and instruments (see Table 16). Duties on semi-manufactured goods were slightly lowered. The increased selectivity in manufacturing products went by largely unnoticed. The public debate concentrated on agricultural tariffs. Whereas grain prices were below world market prices in the early 1920's and after the stabilization, the demand for tariff protection by agricultural lobbies came at a time of already rising grain prices which reached their peak in 1925. The opposition of the center and of social democrats who represented consumer interests was not strong enough to block the reinstatement of grain tariffs, but their level was below the 1902 Bülow tariff.

159. In the period 1925-1929 tariff policy changed very little. Falling world market prices at constant specific tariffs, however, constituted rising grain protection [Gerschenkron, 1943, p. 133]. Costs of production declined in the United States and Canada through the introduction of the tractor, the combine, and dry-farming. Together with increasing

(1) The RDI, founded in 1919, was the overall umbrella organization of German industry. It arose from the unification of CDI and BdI. The conflicts between the previous two organizations continued inside RDI, however.

Table 16 - Tariff levels in Germany, 1913, 1927, and 1931 (in percent)(a)

	1913		1927		1931	
	min	max	min	max	min	max
Foodstuffs (b)	27.4	29.3	29.6	35.6	78.5	89.0
Semimanufactured goods (c)	13.2	17.5	10.4	18.6	19.0	27.8
Manufactured industrial goods	8.5	11.7	15.5	22.7	15.0	21.6
of which:						
textiles	10.0	14.5	21.0	43.0	26.0	45.0
metal goods	6.7	13.0	9.5	15.0	12.5	18.5
machines	4.3	14.2	3.7	15.0	3.7	15.0
vehicles	3.3	8.2	24.0	40.0	8.8	22.0
instruments	6.0	6.0	19.0	19.5	20.0	20.0

(a) Estimated ad valorem equivalents to specific duties. - (b) Excluding alcoholic beverages and tobacco. - (c) Excluding mineral oils.

Source: Liepmann [1938, p. 383].

exports from Russia, prices reacted strongly especially after 1928 [Röpke, 1934, p. 57]. In 1927 agricultural protection in Germany was higher than in neighboring countries [Liepmann, 1938, p. 113]. This development ended in an ad valorem equivalent tariff of over 80 percent in 1931, for some grains such as rye of up to 300 percent.

160. The world economic crisis brought about the final turn of German trade policy toward near autarchy in foodstuffs, while semi-manufactured goods protection was raised from 10.4-18.6 percent in 1927 to 19.0-27.8 percent in 1931 and industrial goods protection remained about constant at 15.5-22.8 percent in 1927 and 15.0-21.6 percent in 1931. Again, a coincidence of several factors made this trade policy change possible. Because of the increasing world production of grain and the beginning decline of grain prices most governments - including the United States with the Smoot-Hawley Act of 1930 - resorted to protection in order to help their agricultural clientele, thus increasingly turning world grain markets into residual markets with accelerating downward movement of prices. As ad valorem grain tariffs started to rise, worldwide surplus grain pressed prices down. Subsequently governments increased tariff levels to maintain internal grain price stability.

161. In this spiral tariffs were raised to unprecedented levels, but agricultural incomes could not be maintained in Germany. In 1929, the leading agricultural organizations got together and formed the "Grüne Front" (Green Front). For the first time since World War I, a united agricultural lobby – organized across party lines – started to influence the parliamentary process. The intense agitation – inside and outside parliament – of the Grüne Front did succeed; not least since the SPD, in its 1927 congress in Kiel, abandoned its strict advocacy of consumer interests in favor of a grain monopoly which would "serve the interests of both consumers and producers primarily by pursuing a policy of price stabilization". The underlying idea of the program was that an understanding between industrial workers and peasants was a necessary safeguard of democracy [Gerschenkron, 1943, p. 128 f.]. Although the agrarian program did not explicitly support agrarian tariffs, the social democratic government during the second half of 1929 increased grain tariffs by almost 100 percent.

162. Whereas the East-Elbian Junkers were for a short time relieved from international competition, effective protection of cattle and dairy farmers diminished drastically. In order to prevent the collapse of farmers producing high-grade products parallel tariff increases became necessary for virtually all agricultural products. In addition, quota regulations and other measures such as the "Vermahlungszwang" which forced German flour-mills to use a certain percentage of German wheat, the government monopoly of maize, or the dying of rye to prevent it from entering the market for human consumption had been introduced [Röpke, 1934, p. 58]. With this host of interventions, the German Government isolated the domestic grain market almost entirely from the world market; home production increased to make Germany practically self-sufficient in bread grains.

163. Agrarian protection, however, did not succeed in stabilizing domestic grain prices or agricultural incomes. After early attempts of open-market interventions failed due to a lack of financial resources, the measures mentioned dramatically increased the price differences between German and world-market prices to over 200 percent for wheat and al-

Figure 2 - German and World Market Prices for Grains, 1927-1939 (RM/1000 kg)

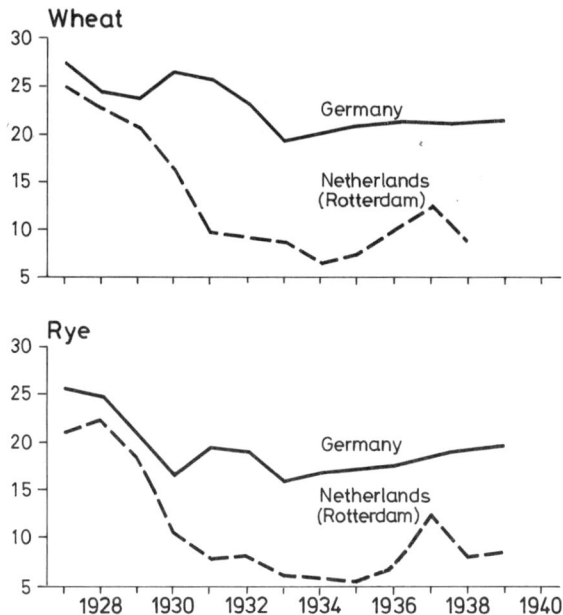

Source: Statistisches Reichsamt [various issues].

most 200 percent for rye in 1934 (1)(Figure 2). Nevertheless, the downward trend in domestic prices was not be stopped. Between 1927 and 1933 wheat prices fell from 27.33 RM/1000 kg to 19.18 RM/1000 kg and rye prices fell from 25.03 RM/1000 kg to 15.73 RM/1000 kg. Between 1925 and 1933, on the other hand, industrial wages remained about constant. The average salary for one shift in coal mining was 6.90 RM in 1925 and 6.92 RM in 1933. In the same period, annual per-capita incomes in agriculture fell from 582 RM to 447 RM [Statistisches Reichsamt, 1925-1933]. The relative position of agriculture deteriorated during this period. This may also explain, why - despite the dramatic sectoral protection of agriculture - farmers were not satisfied with the governments at that time and in large portions turned to the National Socialists in 1932.

_____

(1) Measured as the difference between the German average price and the price in Rotterdam in percent of the Rotterdam price [Statistisches Reichsamt, 1936].

164. When Hitler came to power in 1933 international trade relations were already at a low ebb. Protection proliferated and bilateralism became the dominating form of conducting trade relations. The American Reciprocal Trade Agreement Act (1934), the British Import Duties Act (1932), and the "Neue Plan" or "Schacht Plan" (1934) (noted in Figure 1) by the German government are evidence for this swing to bilateralism. In Germany, the National Socialists completed what previous governments had started: the total control of foreign trade. Industrial and agricultural organizations became centralized. The control of agriculture was taken over by the "Reichsnährstand" (Reich Food Estate) which at the same time was a government monopoly administrating foreign trade and domestic prices and it was the unified organization of farmers.

Soon the logic of "Kriegswirtschaft" (war economy) took over and bilateral trade was conducted according to the preferences of the National-Socialist leaders. Export subsidies and export cartels were introduced to promote the export of finished products in order to finance imports of raw materials and strategic military goods. A complex administrative structure developed which added to the inefficiency of administered prices. Germany's import share of GDP dropped from some 15 percent in the late 1920's to about 6 percent after 1934. Economic considerations more and more disappeared. Hitler commented at the annual party convention in Nuremberg in September 1936: "I consider it necessary that now 100 percent autarky will be established with iron resolution in all areas in which it is feasible ... . The German economy must be ready for war in 4 years." [Cited in Fischer, 1961, p. 76: authors' translation].

6. Germany's Return to the World Market

165. There are only a few cases in history where there is a chance to redesign thoroughly trade institutions and trade policy. The end of World War II provided this chance internationally, as well as nationally for Germany. Why did Germany not establish a free-trade system? After all, the autarchic prewar policies were discredited. In this case too, a

mixture of domestic and foreign policy goals conflicted. On the national level one would expect ample opportunities for a rational new beginning after the unconditional capitulation. Yet, interest groups formed faster than administrations and the parliamentary system. Consequently the constellation of domestic interests came out similar to that before World War II (and even World War I), but of course the international constraints facing Germany were far different.

a. Allied Objectives

166. When an end to World War II came in sight in 1944, the governments of the United States, Great Britain, and the USSR had already decided to put the authority over Germany in the hands of the Allied Control Council, composed of the chiefs of staff of the three countries – it was joined by France on May 1, 1945. The Allied Control Council was designed to decide on matters concerning Germany as a whole – under the directives of the national governments. The division of Germany into occupation zones, the principle of unanimity for decisions in the Allied Control Council, and the provision that in cases of disagreement each occupying force could act independently in its zone, were crucial decisions on Germany's way back to sovereignty. Apart from the measures taken in the Allied Control Council, each country became active in its own zone.

167. American interests and goals were laid down in three documents: the Joint Chiefs of Staff directive (JCS) 1067, the Executive Committee on Economic Foreign Policy (ECEFP) D-61/45, and the Informal Policy Committee on Germany (IPCOG) 2 [cf. Jerchow, 1979, Appendix]. The central document is the JCS 1067, in which the political goals as well as the immediate measures to be taken after the occupation were formulated. With respect to foreign trade the Americans expected the Control Council to "establish centralized control over all trade in goods and services with foreign countries" (JCS 1067, § 40). For the American zone foreign trade was restricted so as to ensure that "imports which are permitted and furnished to Germany are confined to those unavoidably necessary to the objectives stated in paragraphs 4 and 5", and that "exports to countries

other than the United Nations are prohibited unless specifically autho-
rized by the Allied governments" (JCS 1067, § 41).

168. Whereas JCS 1067 was concerned with the immediate postwar situation, the ECEFP prepared a document outlining the long range perspectives on German foreign trade. In the so-called ECEFP D-61/45, the main
objective of American economic policy in Germany consisted of preventing
the participation of Germans in international cartels, which was thought
to be a safeguard against any quick economic recovery of Germany. The
ECEFP expected a complete breakdown of German foreign trade after the
capitulation. Later - it was expected - any emerging trade should be
conducted between the administration of the Occupying Forces and foreign governments. An agency under allied control which could administer
and control Germany's foreign trade in the interest of the Allied nations
was proposed. The Joint Export-Import Agency (JEIA) realized this idea
for the Bizone (the British and American zones combined) in January
1947.

169. Finally, the IPCOG, which had drafted JCS 1067, prepared a document containing the American objectives regarding reparations and res-
titution. This document - IPCOG 2 - made very it clear that, parallel to
the political interests of the United States with respect to Germany, the
economic interests of American export industry were to be secured in all
decisions on foreign trade. The provisions of IPCOG 2 were designed to
limit, as far as possible, the flow of German finished products, in the
form of reparations or commercial exports, to the world market. Yet, at
the same time, the cost of the Occupation Forces and any US shipments
- mainly foodstuffs - should be financed by Germany through exports.
These two conflicting provisions reflected diverging interests in the
American administration and eventually forced new and clearer policy
decisions upon the US government.

170. The British government was faced with the same dilemma, though
more directly than the US government. It was believed that an economically strong Germany was essential for a well-functioning and
profitable European market, favorable to the British export industry and
the British treasury. On the other hand, the administration did not want

Germany's exports to compete with the British. The compromise was essentially the same as the American decisions: Germany should be allowed to export just enough to pay for the expenditures of the Allies.

171. France was not so much concerned with concrete economic objectives, since she was focusing on dividing Germany into small independent units. With such a policy de Gaulle had expected to lay the ground for France to become a hegemonical power in Western Europe and, at the same time, to prevent Germany from ever again becoming a threat to French interests, military or economic.

172. These were essentially the ideas and objectives of the Western Allies when they took command of their respective zones. However, when confronted with reality in Germany and with the policies of other countries, each had to adjust her objectives as well as her policy measures over the following months and years.

b. After Capitulation

173. The Allied Control Council issued Proclamation No. 2 in September 1945; it took away Germany's sovereignty for all external contacts, economic, political and diplomatic, foreign trade had already begun under Allied Control. The first investigations, ordered by OMGUS (Office of Military Government United States, Berlin), predicted starvation, epidemics, and disorder. By broad interpretation of JCS 1067 §5, General Clay, the Deputy Military Governor for Germany, ordered the import of more than 950 000 tons of wheat from June to December 1945 [Jerchow, 1978, p. 149] for the American and British zones. In Washington there were obvious misconceptions about the extent of destruction in Germany. Members of the OMGUS in Berlin, however, clearly saw the need for initiatives beyond the spirit of the political directives coming from Washington. Since food imports were expected to continue in 1946 and 1947, the allied authorities in Germany had to find ways of financing these imports. To use American of British taxpayers' money was not feasible politically. Therefore OMGUS made clear to the newly founded "Länderrat": "For payment of imports, balance of exports are essential." [ibid.,

p. 353]. The "Länderrat" was asked to prepare an export-production program and submit it to OMGUS "to provide sufficient funds to meet the obligations arising from imports of food, merchandise, raw materials and supplies currently required for minimum subsistence" [American Military Government Regulations, Title 13-302, cited in Jerchow, 1978, p. 369].

174. Not only the immediate financial interests of the United States as the main food supplier were important. France depended on imports of German coal. Ninety-four percent of all exports from the British zone between August and December 1945 consisted of coal [Jerchow, 1978, p. 341]. Exports from the French zone were also dominated by raw materials and intermediate inputs [ibid., p. 166]. All foreign trade was conducted through the allied military administrations and export prices were set significantly below world market levels. Whereas France and Britain, at least in the short run, seemed to benefit from such a situation by buying below world market prices, the United States lost. That country had to supply the food aid which was only to a small extent paid for by German exports and she did not gain from their underpricing. This apparent discrepancy between economic and political interests was immediately recognized in the OMGUS and much later in Washington. Consequently, the OMGUS was more favorable towards an expansion and liberalization of German exports than the Allies and Washington, but would not precommit itself to a unilateral solution.

c. The Joint-Export-Import Agency (JEIA) Era

175. Despite ongoing negotiations in the Control Council and by the Allied Foreign Ministers for a unified Germany, "by the spring of 1946 much of this optimism has gone" [Gimbel, 1968, p. 52] as General Lucius Clay wrote. In spring and summer 1946 the United States went ahead to establish the Bizone. In the Bevin-Byrnes Treaty of December 2, 1946, balanced trade by 1949 was envisaged. The JEIA was founded and became responsible for the administration of foreign trade. In the beginning, all contracts with foreign countries were made by the JEIA. The Dollar Clause required that all German exports be paid in US dollars, a condition under which many countries - short of dollars themselves -

were not willing to trade with Germany. This policy Erhard called the most damaging for German recovery [Erhard, 1954, p. 81]. In the course of the next two years the JEIA increasingly delegated authority to German exporters and to the German administration.

176. After the Currency Reform of 1948 artificial export and import prices - set by the JEIA and the French administration in their own favor - were replaced by the exchange rate DM3.33 per US dollar and partial convertibility. In December 1948 the JEIA permitted direct trading negotiations of German businessmen with their foreign customers. Foreign trade expanded considerably in this period [Gimbel, 1968, p. 230].

177. The political factors leading to this change are manifold. Severe economic problems in Britain and France naturally made the United States an economic and political leader. The political process in the United States, therefore, dominated Allied policies in the western zones. In Washington, economic policies were discussed in a wider political context. The beginning of the Cold War on the one hand and the financial burden of the economic recovery program for Western Europe on the other hand became the background for decisions regarding the Bizone and later the Trizone. One cannot single out any one argument as being decisive for this policy change from JCS/1067 and other documents to active recovery programs and liberalization. Yet, economic as well as political considerations pointed in the same direction:

- The establishment of civil governments and administrations in the Soviet zone as early as in summer 1945 was feared as supportive of socialist tendencies in the western zones. To stop the communist threat economically and politically, decentralized zones were seen as the appropriate measures. Economic policies, therefore, were oriented towards the establishment and strengthening of a market economy without cartels or large conglomerates. In general, European recovery - it was hoped - would lead to the "eventual unification of Germany by drawing the Soviet zone into the West with the economic magnet of higher production, better living standards, and the like; possible attraction of Czechoslovakia and Poland by this same economic magnet" [Gimbel, 1968, p. 163/4].

- Economic considerations were dominated by the overwhelming interests of all Western Allies in a quick European recovery. The concerns of American taxpayers were sharply formulated in Congress. The administration, therefore, designed the Marshall Plan so as to achieve a quick recovery. Gimbel [1968, p. 166] summarizes the view of the President's committee on Foreign Policy that "the American desire for German recovery and the economic needs of Europe dovetailed neatly, provided that political-military factors were not ignored. It said that, in the main, other countries needed German metals, machinery and chemicals to attain self-sufficiency". During the Marshall Plan hearings in June 1948 Marshall himself stated that German recovery was so essential for the rest of Western Europe that the United States would go ahead without a four-power agreement.

d. Constrained Sovereignty

178. When the Allied High Commission returned de facto sovereignty in trade policy to the German Federal Government in November 1949 (1), West Germany's return to the world market was already prepared by several decisions under JEIA authority. Although the von Bülow tariff of 1902 remained in force, the completely centralized trade contracts by the JEIA had resulted in bilateral quota systems laid down in trade treaties with almost 50 countries by late 1949. Only in rare cases were tariffs charged on the price-controlled imports. This system was used by the German government to conduct bilateral trade policy.

179. During the first GATT Round in Geneva the occupying countries granted unconditional MFN status to all imports on the basis of the old von Bülow tariff. This "Statement of Annecy", amounting to a unilateral liberalization, was harshly criticized in the German public. Even Ludwig Erhard called it a "servitude" comparable to the treatment of Germany in the treaty of Versailles: [Erhard, 1954, p. 210]. Yet, even before the "Statement of Annecy", the Bipartite Control Office (BICO) had already

---

(1) De jure, the AHC still signed all trade treaties. This was abandoned in March, 1951, with Directive No. 6 of the High Commission.

warned that the conditions for West Germany's entering the GATT - the
Geneva Agreement - were not met, since "some of the existing German
tariff rates do constitute significant barriers to trade and, therefore,
the assumption on which the agreement is based are to that extent not
satisfied" (1). This initiated several rounds of haggling over a list of
tariff preferences between the BICO and the "Vereinigte Wirtschaftsrat".
Finally, in April 1950, the BICO succeeded in pushing through the list
of tariff preferences for West Germany.

180. Parallel to West Germany's integration in international organizations
the JEIA had designated the Bizone as a leader in trade liberalization
inside the Organization for European Economic Cooperation (OEEC). On
November 2, 1949, the member states agreed to remove quotas on
50 percent of their imports within six weeks. Germany continued in leading liberalization and reached - interrupted by the "Liberalisierungsstop"
in early 1951 - a "Liberalisierungsquote" of 90 percent in spring 1953.
Overall, about two thirds of German imports were free of quotas by 1952
[Erhard, 1954, p. 116]. Whereas Erhard attributed this leadership role
to the free-trade orientation in the German government, others point to
the political pressure of the JEIA Administration as the moving force.

181. In this situation of limited sovereignty for West Germany and a lack
of consensus inside West Germany about the principles of a future trade
policy, a new tariff code had to be written for economic as well as political reasons. A prerequisite for Germany's participation in the GATT
conference on trade liberalization in Torquay was the enactment of a
tariff code which was not to be a bargaining tariff. The von Bülow tariff
of 1902 was inappropriate for several reasons:

- It was a specific tariff. Since relative prices and industrial structure
  had changed, the ad valorem equivalent rates could not represent any
  trade policy interests at all.

- Most countries' tariff schedules used the Brussels Tariff Nomenclature.
  For tariff negotiations West Germany needed a comparable tariff
  schedule.

(1) BICO/Memo (48) 84; cited in Jerchow [1979, p. 259].

- A new tariff would allow Germany regain room for manoever, since unconditional MFN treatment had been granted to third countries in the Statement of Annecy on the basis of the von Bülow tariff. The "Zolltarifausschuss" (Tariff Commission) explicitly stated: this Statement "kann nur durch einen neuen Zolltarif überwunden werden." [BMWi, a, p. 8].

182. The other member states of the OEEC naturally expected Germany to be the leader in tariff concessions because of her lack of political influence. They also watched very critically the formulation of the new tariff schedule. The open-door policy of the US Administration nicely matched European interests. The "Zolltarifausschuss", therefore, faced a number of constraints, some explicitly written down, some implicit:

- According to the Geneva agreement (November 1949) the new tariff was not to be a bargaining tariff. The German government, therefore, decided to design the new schedule roughly according to the tariff levels of 1937. This constraint alone would not have been very strong, since 1937 tariff levels were extraordinarily high (Figure 1).

- The prohibition of a bargaining tariff also forced the "Zolltarifausschuss" to consider other European countries' tariff levels. It was to stay below the average European tariff level [ibid., p. 13]. An indication of the political force of this constraint is the 180-page appendix the Zolltarifausschuss added to its proposal with a tariff-line-by-tariff-line comparison of the new German tariffs with those of the United States, the United Kingdom, France, Italy, and the Benelux [BMWi, b].

183. The "Zolltarifausschuss" was set up by the federal governments and it consisted of 13 members [BMWi, 1950a, p. 8]: seven representatives from federal and state governments, three from the "Arbeitsgemeinschaft Außenhandel" - one each from industry, retailers, and crafts - two from agriculture, and one from the trade unions. The unequal representation of certain sectors is evident. Three representatives were directly pro-agriculture; two state government representatives came from rural states. Consumers were not represented officially, but the representative of the trade unions supported consumer interests. In general, the DGB

112

favored tariff levels about 50 percent lower than those of the proposed tariff schedule [Jerchow, 1979, p. 270].

184. Given the international constraints, the formulation of the tariff was dominated by special interest groups with a protectionist bias. The average European tariff level was not surpassed, but some sectors obtained above average protection. Agriculture succeeded in getting high tariffs, yet her effective protection was lowered by high tariffs on fertilizer supported by the chemical industry and trade unions. Similarly, the textile industry, the steel industry, and the chemical industry were able to establish their desired tariff levels.

185. Consequently, the AHC, whose approval was required, accepted the average tariff level as sufficiently low, but criticized the too frequent use of the maximum tariff of 35 percent; the "Zolltarifausschuss" had chosen to underline "the liberal nature of the tariff reform" [BMWi, a]. The AHC specifically ordered lower tariffs for several agricultural products, for iron, aluminum, and steel products, for several textile products, and for all chemicals. Subsequent negotiations between the German Government and the AHC were accompanied by intense lobbying of the criticized industries. In its first statement, even the Ministry of Economics hinted that, if the AHC were to insist on its demands, West Germany might be as well off renouncing participation in Torquay and keeping its new tariff schedule [ibid., p. 273 f.]. Finally the German Government made a few concessions and the tariff was sent to the member states of GATT with the proviso "to reexamine certain of the proposed rates." [ibid., p. 276].

186. It is evident that the politico-economic process inside Germany resulted in a tariff which "is more strongly protectionist than was the old even in its prime" [Wallich, 1955, p. 258], given the international constraints set by GATT rules and the AHC. Of course, from this one cannot deduce that West Germany was protectionist. After all, the tariff was considered a bargaining tariff only. Yet, there were protectionist groups in Germany, most notably agriculture, textiles, steel, and the chemical industries. For them, the tariff code can be considered a success. Even, if there were major tariff concessions in the GATT negotia-

tions, the sectoral structure of protection would most likely favor then, although at a lower level (1). The discussion in the German government and the German public during the formulation of the tariff and thereafter made clear that there was no consensus on a truly liberal trading regime. A majority was for modest liberalization, and proponents of a unilateral move towards free trade could not find resonance in the government, nor the parliament, nor the public.

e. Reintegration

187. The last steps towards reintegration into the world trading system came in April, 1951, when the protocol of Torquay was signed, and in October, 1951 when West Germany became an official member of GATT. During the ensuing years, the quota system was abandoned step by step as planned in the OEEC. German trade policy during the Korea Boom was determined by the unexpected success of her export industry. Unilateral liberalization steps were believed to be the best form of export promotion [Erhard, 1955, p. 244]. Agriculture, however, was exempted from this process, as was the coal and steel complex. This liberalization was not only considered a sign of goodwill, it also was forced by the constrained convertibility of the Deutsche mark where trade was conducted on bilateral trade accounts. The large surpluses on some of these accounts amounted to a waste of resources. Since convertibility was not in sight, lower import barriers saved export credits and facilitated bilateral trade.

---

(1) Incidentally, there has not been that much change in the tariff structure over the last 40 years. See Chapters I and II.

VI. Trade Policy and International Competitiveness of Industries

1. Introduction

188. Whatever the motives for the mixed assortment of trade and industrial policies actually undertaken in West Germany, the question naturally
arises whether the policies have had any impact on trade flows. Because
the policies quantified in this study do discriminate among industries,
they can be expected to exert an influence on the international competitiveness of industries located in West Germany. In order to isolate their
effect, the natural, or nontrade policy, causes need to be controlled.
Interindustry trade among countries with noticeably different is relatively well explained by the factor proportions hypothesis provided human
capital is recognized as a separate factor of production (1).

189. As poorer countries have grown faster than richer ones since World
War II, relative factor endowments of countries have become more similar
(2). At the same time, intraindustry trade has grown faster than interindustry trade [see Balassa, 1966; Grubel, Lloyd, 1975]. This empirical
phenomenon has been one element motivating a research program seeking
to explain the commodity composition of international trade among similar
countries. That program - the Strategic Trade Theory Program - focuses
on scale economies internal to the firm, and hence market structure, as
an independent explanation of trade flows. It has antecedents in what
Krugman [1987] approvingly calls the "counter-culture" of international
trade, such as Vernon's [1966] product cycle explanation for trade,

---

(1) This emerged in the wake of Leontief's [1954] famous paradox,
especially through the work of Kenen [1965]. An early survey of
empirical results in Stern [1975]. See Weiss [1983] for a survey of
research on West Germany's trade, and Deardorff [1985] for a
survey of research on the United States' trade. Leamer [1984]
throws cold water on the strict consistency of the empirical evidence
with a more than two factor Heckscher-Ohlin model, but it still holds
up as an empirical regularity and may not be so far from what the
model predicts in any case [Anderson, 1988].

(2) The facts are not in dispute. The "catch-up" hypothesis attributes
part of the more rapid growth to the lower initial level of income of
the poorer countries [see Abramovitz, 1986; Baumol, 1986; Heitger,
1987].

which eventually pointed to R&D expenditures as determining competitiveness. Trade theory pointing to economies of scale and market structure as determinants of trade flows has been thin on prediction of the precise commodity composition of international trade, but thick on predictions of other characteristics of industries and firms that determine the gains from trade.

190. Following Markusen and Venables [1986], it might be fair to summarize the results of strategic trade theory according to two criteria (1). One is that if markets are segmented a trade barrier can improve welfare by driving down import prices and expanding domestic output while driving firms down their average cost curves. Another, perhaps more relevant criterion, is that under free entry of firms, trade policy measures - be they tariffs or subsidies - tend to cause entry and so lead to the dissipation of rents. More firms produce so that they move "up the average cost curve" [Horstmann, Markusen, 1986]. In contrast, if the number of firms is fixed, a policy measure targeted to one of the firms can increase the firm's output and profits (2). It would be wrong to think that strategic trade theory implies that governments should use trade policy in this manner. On the contrary, the theory identifies and formalizes additional sources of gains from trade in the presence of scale economies when trade is liberalized [see especially Helpman, Krugman, 1985], namely the pro-competitive effect of trade. Thus the case for multilateral trade barrier reductions to improve world welfare is strengthened. For present purposes, the predictions of the theory about firm size and a few other industry characteristics in the presence of policy measures can be confronted with the facts for West Germany. Thus, there is no attempt here at competitive testing of trade theories, as factor proportions theory still has much to predict in the presence of differences in factor endowments and in the absence of imperfect competition in some industries [Helpman, Krugman, 1985]. Besides, as Johnson wrote of another set of seemingly rival trade theories and "the artificiality of the rival-hypothesis-testing approach" [Johnson, 1975,

---

(1) See also Venables [1985], Grossman and Richardson [1985], Deardorff [1985], and Venables and Smith [1986].
(2) Especially clear examples are Brander and Spencer's R&D subsidies [1983] and export subsidies [1985].

p. 47]: "Every blind man who touches a part of the elephant learns some of the truth about it - but not the whole truth; and only the rare unfortunate is unlucky enough to be caught in generalizing about the elephant from an unrepresentative handhold on the tip of its tail".

2. Protection and Comparative Advantage

191. The interindustry structure of industries' competitiveness needs to be measured in such a way that the effect of macroeconomic variables which impinge upon the trade balance is allowed for. One such measure is Liesner's [1958] and Balassa's [1967] concept of Revealed Comparative Advantage (RCA). The version chosen here is:

$$RCA = \ln \left[(x_i/m_i) / \left(\sum_k x_k / \sum_k m_k \right) \right]$$

where x and m refer to exports and imports respectively, and the indices run over industries at a point in time.

192. These values were calculated for West German industries trade with the total world and for selected regions in the mid-1970's and the mid-1980's. The results are shown in Table 17. It is immediately apparent that - overall - the interindustry structure of competitiveness changed very little. This even applies to the industries identified in Chapter II as objects of pronounced trade or industrial policy - coal mining, iron and steel, aircraft, data processing equipment, and textiles and clothing - changed but little in RCA values. Indeed, some gained and some lost in competitiveness. Traditionally strong German export industries, such as mechanical engineering and road vehicles declined slightly, but precision mechanics, ceramic products and electrical engineering declined more noticeably. The relative changes in each industry's position is much more pronounced in trade with Japan and trade with the LDC's than in trade with the total world.

Table 17 - Revealed Comparative Advantage of West German Industries, 1978 and 1985

I-O Sec-tor	Industry	World 1978	World 1985	Japan 1978	Japan 1985	LDC's 1978	LDC's 1985
6	coal mining	-2.56	-2.44	3.86	5.18	-4.09	-5.42
	Manufacturing intermediate goods						
9	chemicals	0.35	0.14	1.26	1.32	1.74	1.37
10	petroleum refining	-1.65	-2.19	1.57	0.89	-1.44	-3.29
12	rubber goods	-0.04	-0.20	-0.31	-0.09	1.40	0.32
13	stone goods	-0.85	-0.19	-0.35	-0.26	-0.14	0.51
16	iron and steel	-0.14	0.13	-3.59	-0.96	1.29	0.98
17	nonferrous metals	-1.28	-0.76	1.33	2.13	-2.76	-1.37
18	foundries	0.15	0.30	-2.21	-0.72	1.78	1.96
19	drawing mills, cold rolling mills	0.56	0.37	-0.98	-0.40	3.36	1.36
30	wood	-1.58	-0.98	-1.20	2.21	-3.72	-2.88
32	pulp, paper, paperboard	-1.46	-0.88	1.72	1.29	1.76	-0.19
	investment goods						
20	structural engineering, rolling stock	0.32	0.81	1.81	2.21	2.22	2.75
21	mechanical engineering	1.16	0.95	1.44	0.74	4.22	2.87
22	electronic data processing equipment	0.17	-0.23	0.57	-1.68	1.55	-0.95
23	road vehicles	1.06	0.89	1.11	-1.10	3.61	2.19
24	shipbuilding	0.50	0.29	-4.59	-3.80	3.80	0.39
25	aircraft, aerospace	-1.16	-0.44	-3.33	1.73	0.62	0.02
26	electrical engineering	0.54	0.10	-1.14	-1.27	1.71	0.37
27	precision mechanics, optics, watches	0.53	0.04	-0.74	-0.84	1.41	0.36
28	metal products	0.81	0.41	-0.42	0.20	2.11	0.76
	consumer goods						
11	plastic products	0.33	0.19	-0.58	-0.21	0.15	0.20
14	ceramic products	0.33	-0.23	-2.34	-0.22	2.10	-0.44
15	glass and glass products	-0.25	-0.06	-0.04	1.74	1.35	0.31
29	musical instruments, toys, sporting goods, jewellery	-0.77	-0.24	-1.71	-0.14	-2.30	-1.55
31	wood products	-0.38	-0.23	-1.19	1.93	-1.54	0.56
33	paper and paperboard products	0.04	0.32	-1.03	0.59	1.80	1.18
34	printing	0.70	0.69	1.76	0.93	1.69	1.38
35	leather, leather goods, shoes	-1.32	-1.35	-0.23	1.08	-2.66	-2.71
36	textiles	-0.90	-0.55	-0.43	0.28	-2.16	-1.86
37	clothing	-1.25	-1.06	-1.97	1.08	-3.87	-3.50

Source: Calculated from Statistisches Bundesamt [d].

193. The factor proportions approach to explaining interindustry trade flows works where factor proportions differ substantially among countries and human capital is recognized as a separate factor of production [Kenen, 1965]. Here, this factor was computed as the capitalized difference between wages and salaries per employee and the wage of unskilled workers [Fels, 1972]. The results of regressions to explain the interindustry pattern of competitiveness by human and physical capital intensity are shown in Table 18. They are - not without reason - only partly convincing. The evidence is certainly consistent with the observation that West Germany is still a relatively capital rich country, but in trade with the world as a whole the explained variation is low. Factor proportions alone explain nothing about German-Japanese bilateral trade. Only in trade with the LDC's do the hypotheses have any explanatory power worth noting, a by now often found result [see, e.g., Fels, 1972]. This outcome should not be too surprising given the relatively small difference in per capita incomes and hence relative resource endowments between West Germany and the larger trading partners.

194. While this is an unpromising start in trying to control natural determinants of the interindustry structure of trade flows, German effective protection rates were added to the regressions. These were statistically insignificant and of an unexpected sign, another by now common result. One cause for this problem may be that other countries' structures of protection are codetermining trade outcomes in a systematic way, and if these could be included in the analysis, the statistical results would be more convincing. For the case of West Germany's bilateral trade with Japan this was made possible by the availability of Shouda's [1987] effective tariff protection calculation for the pre-Tokyo Round and the post-Tokyo Round periods. The statistical analysis was undertaken not because relative bilateral trade balances have any welfare significance, but because it seems like a conceivable way to isolate the effect of trade policy on trade flows. These rates, insofar as they could reasonably be assigned to the German industrial classification, are shown in Table 19. The interindustry structure of effective tariff protection in Japan is not so different from that of other mature industrial countries. Raw material intensive good, including food and beverages, are protected more than most industries. The usefulness of the tariff protection

Table 18 - Revealed Comparative Advantage as a Function of Selected
Determinants of International Trade, 1978 and 1985 -
Regression Results (a)

Equa-tion	Region/country	Constant	Exogenous variables(b)		$\bar{R}^2$	F
			1978			
[1]	World	-7.13 (-1.71)	+0.80 HUM CAP (2.12*)	-0.14 PHYS CAP (-0.50)	0.09	2.29
[2]	Japan	-8.75 (-1.96)	+0.28 HUM CAP (0.34)	+0.46 PHYS CAP (-0.72)	-0.04	0.47
[3]	LDC's	-36.62 (-3.78*)	+3.40 HUM CAP (3.87*)	+0.08 PHYS CAP (0.11)	0.37	8.82*
			1985			
[4]	World	-6.97 (-1.96)	+0.71 HUM CAP (2.46*)	-0.12 PHYS CAP (-0.54)	0.13	3.06*
[5]	Japan	8.44 (0.94)	-0.63 HUM CAP (-0.87)	-0.06 PHYS CAP (-0.10)	-0.04	0.46
[6]	LDC's	-27.15 (-3.00*)	+2.26 HUM CAP (3.10*)	+0.06 PHYS CAP (0.10)	0.25	5.46*

(a) Cross-section of industries; manufacturing industries, oil refining excluded (N=28); t-values in parentheses; * significant at the 5 percent level. - (b) All variables in natural logarithms; Revealed Comparative Advantage (RCA), see text; HUM CAP = human capital, PHYS CAP = physical capital.

Source: Statistisches Bundesamt [d; e]; Baumgart et al. [various issues].

estimates for further analysis might seem to be limited by the widely discussed apparent prevalence in Japan of other border measures and financial assistance. This is not the place to enter into that discussion (1). Suffice it to say that industrial policy measures in Japan appear to be uncorrelated with tariff protection across industries [Heitger, Stehn, 1988] (2). The results of the new regressions are shown in Table 20.

(1) See e.g. Balassa [1987] and Saxonhouse [1984] for opposing views.
(2) Staiger, Deardorff, Stern [1987] present some tariff equivalents of NTB's in Japan. A comparison of their Table 2 with Table 19 above confirms this impression.

Table 19 - Effective Tariff Protection in Japan, 1972-1987 (a)

I-O Sector	Industry	1972	1975	1987
1,2	Agriculture, forestry, fisheries	2.8	4.9	6.7
6-8	Mining	-0.7	-0.7	-0.5
	Manufacturing	14.4	25.3	22.0
9	chemicals	8.8	15.4	11.6
10	petroleum refining	7.1	12.6	19.2
12,part35	rubber goods, leather goods	12.3	16.9	14.1
13	stone goods	8.1	11.6	8.4
16,19	iron and steel, rolling mills	17.1	57.3	19.5
17	nonferrous metals	22.1	30.3	20.8
32	pulp, paper, paperboard	11.0	17.3	9.4
21	mechanical engineering	8.7	8.7	6.2
23,24	road vehicles, shipbuilding	9.2	7.1	2.8
26	electrical engineering	5.4	10.2	7.4
27	precision mechanics, optics, watches	10.4	8.6	6.2
28	metal products	9.9	10.3	6.5
31	wood products	16.1	22.2	18.1
34	printing	-0.9	-8.3	-0.6
36	textiles	18.6	38.6	38.3
38,39	food and beverages	42.8	67.5	103.9

(a) Based on unweighted nominal tariffs. Allocated to German I-O classification where reasonable.

Source: Shouda [1982].

Firstly, for the early period, the factor proportions theory cum human capital is confirmed. Secondly, the respective levels of effective protection exhibit the correct sign. Protection does hold out imports, and it holds out imports more than it hinders exports. For the later period, factor proportions break down, but this is entirely consistent with Japan's rapid catching-up process relative to Germany and other countries. Nevertheless, the German effective protection structure hinders exports from Japan. Finally, the change in Germany's interindustry competitiveness is consistent with the change in Germany's industrial policy (1). The significant negative sign on human capital is - once again - consistent with Japan's relatively rapid growth.

_____

(1) The change in Japanese tariffs has no discernible effect, perhaps because of the increase in the relative importance of NTB's in that country.

Table 20 - Protection and Human Capital as Determinants of West German-Japanese Trade, 1978-1985 - Regression Results (a)

Endogenous variable	Constant	Exogenous variables (b)			$\bar{R}^2$	F
RCA 78 =	−25.28 (−4.88*)	+2.16 HUM CAP (4.84*)	+0.93 ERA G78 (4.94*)	−0.35 EFF PROT J78 (−2.17*)	0.70	19.67*
RCA 85 =	2.02 (0.25)	−0.21 HUM CAP (−0.32)	+0.71 ERA G85 (2.43*)	−0.39 EFF PROT J85 (−1.52)	0.20	3.01
Δ RCA =	24.16 (4.56*)	−2.17 HUM CAP (−4.40*)	+0.61 ΔERA G (2.89*)	+0.15 ΔEFF PROT J (0.36)	0.47	8.00*

(a) Cross-section of industries (N=25). Observations are for those industries for which Japanese tariffs are available; t-values in parentheses; * significant at the 5 percent level. - (b) All variables in natural logarithms. RCA, revealed comparative advantage; HUM CAP, human capital (1978); ERA, total effective assistance in West Germany; EFF PROT J, effective tariff protection in Japan; G, West Germany; J, Japan; Δ change in 1978-1985.

Source: See Tables 8, 17, 18 and 19.

195. The technology-based hypotheses of Vernon and others fared uniformly poorly in explaining the interindustry pattern of competitiveness Statistical tests of the influence of R&D intensity of industries were unsuccessful. Vernon himself [1979] suggested that rapid dissemination of innovations from one country to the next through the channel of the multinational corporation would tend to produce this result for international flows of manufactured goods.

196. The newer theories of international trade are difficult to test across industries on trade data. In the more competitive versions a domestic industrial policy improves welfare by getting domestic producers to move down their average cost curves, i.e. to expand output, attaining a more efficient scale of production. Specific predictions about which country produces which commodity or which product variant, on the other hand, are scarce [Krugman, 1983]. The oligopolistic versions of the newer theories, in turn, do not make predictions about trade flows in all industries, but only in such industries that are characterized by few producers and, by necessity, limited entry.

3. Trade Policy and Industry Characteristics

197. But instead of confronting changes in trade and industrial policy with trade flows, they can be correlated with changes in average firm size across industries. It has been argued that a rise in protection favors inefficient entry by new firms [Horstmann, Markusen, 1986], i.e. these firms move up the average cost curve. The same may be true if competitive pressures from abroad force distinct industries to reduce capacities and discharge employees. If in such a situation industrial policy raises protection, the process of shrinkage is held up and firms – perhaps especially those on a smaller scale – which otherwise would have to stop producing now operate in a less economical range of production. Thus, in analogy to Horstmann and Markusen [1986] one might conceivably speak of "insufficient exit".

198. That such tendencies – less efficient scale of production in highly protected industries – have been at work in West German manufacturing industries is illustrated in Table 21. As can be seen (Equation [1]), the change in average firm size, measured in percent changes in real sales per firm, has been lowest in those industries which have received the highest additional effective assistance since the late 1970's. In addition, another observation is in line with the above hypothesis of inefficient

Table 21 – Firm Size, Efficiency and Effective Rates of Assistance, 1978-1985 – Regression Results (a)

Equ.	Endogenous variables (b)	Constant	Exogenous variables (c)		$\bar{R}^2$	F	N
[1]	ΔFS	= 15.71 (3.89*)	−0.63 (−2.32*)	ΔERA	0.14	5.40*	28
[2]	ΔREL PROD	= 0.77 (28.22*)	−0.003 (−2.49*)	ΔERA	0.17	6.18*	27

(a) Cross-section regression analysis; t-values in parentheses; * significant at the 5 percent level. – (b) ΔFS, percentage change in real sales per firm, 1978-1985; ΔREL PROD, relative growth of labor productivity of small to large firms, 1978-1985. – (c) ΔERA, change in effective rate of assistance 1978-1985 in percent.

Source: Calculated from Table 8; Statistisches Bundesamt [b; g].

entry (or exit). If one compares labor productivity changes in small versus large firms by industries, the relative productivity growth of small firms in an industry turns out to be smaller, the greater the increase in protection. Both empirical results lend support to the above hypotheses, according to which increases in protection lead to an inefficient scale of production, be it by the entry of new inefficient firms or the insufficient exit of redundant firms.

199. Results for Canadian manufacturing industries support this view [Baldwin, Gorecki, 1983]. They call this the "rationalization effect" of firm exit. Remaining firms expand output and move down the average cost curve. A similar, though not identical, effect may be captured by investment motives of entrepreneurs. For years, the Ifo-Institute in Munich has surveyed German manufacturing firms about the intended consequences of their investment activities, much as McGraw-Hill does for US firms. Three motives are distinguished:

- capacity expansion;

- replacement; and

- rationalization.

A literary juxtaposition of Baldwin and Gorecki's "rationalization effect" with the "rationalization" intent of investment in the Ifo survey would suggest a correlation of changes in protection across industries with the corresponding change in the share of firms reporting a rationalization motive, with the expectation that such a correlation turns out positive. This would be hazardous, however, because rationalization in this context is ill defined (1).

Examination of the survey results shows, however, that the "replacement" motive for investment is rarely reported. The obverse of rationalization, then, is "capacity expansion". While this motive does not necessarily correspond to a static move down the average cost curve, for

---

(1) The concept emerged in Germany in the 1920's (Rationalization Movement) when businesses sought changes in technique which lowered costs, usually administered labor costs. As such, it is always a good thing.

Table 22 - The Relationship between Changes in Effective Assistance
and Industry Characteristics (1978-1985)

Characteristic	Spearman coefficient (a)
Technology	
change in capacity expansion motive (1978-1985)	+0,36*
change in rate of process innovation (1979-1982)	-0,09
change in rate of product innovation (1979-1982)	+0,06
change in R&D expenditures per employee	+0,03
Skill intensity (1978)	
share of high-skilled employees	+0,33*
share of craftspersons	+0,41*
share of low-skilled employees	-0,33*
Physical capital	
physical capital intensity (1978)	+0,24
rate of return (1983)	-0,16
change in the rate of return (1978-1983)	-0,37*
* significant at the 5 percent level. - (a) Of rank correlation.	

Source: Calculated from Table 8 and Statistisches Bundesamt [a; e; f];
Baumgart et al. [1986]; Schmalholz [1985]; Schmidt et al.
[1984]; Echterhoff-Severitt [various issues]; IfO-Institut [1980;
1986].

which investment would not be required, it seems to be a relatively
straightforward concept which might correspond to an intention of increasing optimum plant size, or at least not reducing it. It would seem
to correspond better to the Baldwin and Gorecki [ibid.] concept of
rationalization.

200. Theory is not so well developed here that there is any guidance for
the functional form a test could take. Therefore, Spearman rank correlation coefficients will be used to see whether changes in protection go
hand in hand with changes in cost cutting investments. The striking
results are shown in Table 22. The change in protection is positively
correlated with the change in the share of rationalization investment, and
the size of the correlation means that the result is unlikely to be due to
chance.

201. The Ifo-Institute has recently supplemented its regular annual survey of investment motives with special questions about the extent of product and process innovations [Schmalholz, 1985]. No series long enough for testing the effect of changes in protection on the change in the extent of innovation are available: only the change over a short period can be correlated with the change in protection. Unsurprisingly, the size of the correlations indicates it could well rest on chance. The same applies to changes in R&D expenditures per employee. This is consistent with Vernon's [1979] observation that the location of production and the location of R&D spending no longer have much to do with each other.

202. Apart from these ill effects, the protective system may breed other inefficiencies in factor allocation. In Chapter III it was shown that a large proportion of subsidies was specifically directed to physical capital. Is this institutional bias observable in the data? The answer is yes. While only a low positive correlation between physical capital intensity of industries and the change in protection is discernible (1), increases in protection seem to have gone hand in hand with the decline in the rate of return on physical capital. It is hardly conceivable that increases in protection have caused declines in profitability. One is on surer ground interpreting the causality as running from declining rates of return to increased demand for and supply of protection. This result is entirely consistent with the results of the political economy analysis, though it bears reemphasis that no plausible explanation for so much support of physical capital has emerged.

203. Another set of correlation coefficients seeks to describe how the change in the protective system has been related to the skills of the employed (2); as in the case of physical capital, the results are somewhat surprising. There is weak evidence for discrimination against unskilled labor; weak evidence for the promotion of highly skilled labor; and stronger evidence for the promotion of medium, i.e. craft, skills. Here, too, societal groups are supported by policies which do not fit the

---

(1) The situation is probably typical for Europe. Quantitative evidence for the United Kingdom is given by Metcalf [1984].
(2) This kind of typology rests on Keesing [1965] and Waehrer [1968].

ideology used to justify support. These results are consistent with the observation that it is not the poorest members of society who are being helped, but others. Aside from the social aspect of this problem, this course as a long-run economic proposition is either unsustainable or will go hand in hand with relative, and perhaps absolute, economic decline. Craft skills, old skills, and physical capital are not the factors which lend Europe, least of all Germany, a comparative advantage in anything.

4. Trade Policy in the Steel Industry

204. If one leaves the broad-brush cross sectional examination, something more can be said about the effects of trade policy in individual industries, particularly industries organized in large production units. The steel industry is an important case in point, both in West Germany and in Europe as a whole. It has been made clear that this is a much supported industry, but it is also characterized by a peculiar subsidy cum production quota system. To understand the effect of subsidies, something has to be known about the industrial organization and pricing strategies of the industry. The contention here is that the steel industry can be characterized as a contestable market in the sense of Baumol et al. [1982]. This means that because there are no barriers to entry, pure profits cannot emerge, so that in turn price equals average cost. If there were low enough fixed costs, contestability would converge to perfect competition; if fixed costs were high enough, one firm would supply the world market [Helpman, Krugman, 1985, Ch. 6]. This monopolist could earn no rent because the threat of entry forces him to charge no more than average cost for his product.

205. This description of the steel industry may seem farfetched; hit and run competition, a requirement of contestability, seems difficult. But it should be considered that technology in most steel-making operations has become fairly ubiquitous. In addition, the success of mini-mills suggests that optimal plant size has tended to fall. Thus, if there is sunk cost upon entering steel making, it is likely to be fairly low. Explicit tests of

the structure of the steel industry undertaken by Lont and Mathiesen [1983] and Mathiesen and Wergeland [1986] with a simulation model come to the conclusion that the international steel industry is actually perfectly competitive. Their results are summarized by Haarland and Norman [1987]: "[A simulation model] was constructed on the basis of micro-data on cost functions for different steel-processing techniques in various countries throughout the world. The model was then used to simulate production and trade patterns under alternative assumptions regarding market structure - perfect competition, a general Nash-Cournot equilibrium and a Nash-Cournot equilibrium for some producers with the rest as a competitive fringe. The predicted patterns were confronted with actual world production and trade. The conclusion was that, despite apparently high concentration in the industry, the assumption of perfect competition gave the best fit".

For the present analysis, the weaker form of competition, contestability only, is required.

206. The subsidization cum production quota system that has become prevalent in Europe has another peculiarity that must be recognized. The subsidy is not a subsidy on product output or factor input, but a subsidy on losses. The subsidies are paid by national governments; the EC Commission only legalizes their payment. This makes the subsidy open ended. Firms would have an incentive to produce as much as possible. To limit the extent of subsidization at all in this setup, a system of production quotas is required. The quotas are not allocated to firms on the basis of efficiency considerations, but rather as the outcome of a bargaining process where historic output is an often used argument.

207. This peculiar institutional feature of the steel protection system has important consequences for the social cost of intervention, as illustrated in Figure 3. The average cost curves of two firms are shown, the efficient firm, AC_1, which incurs minimum average cost at world market price p_w, and the inefficient firm, AC_2, which incurs minimum average cost even above the domestic price $p_w(1+t)$. For simplicity each is assigned an identical production quota q^*. Firm 2 requires the subsidy $q^* (AC_2^* - p_w(1+t))$ to maintain operations. Firm 1 is earning a private

Figure 3 - Social Cost under a Production Quota cum Subsidy Scheme

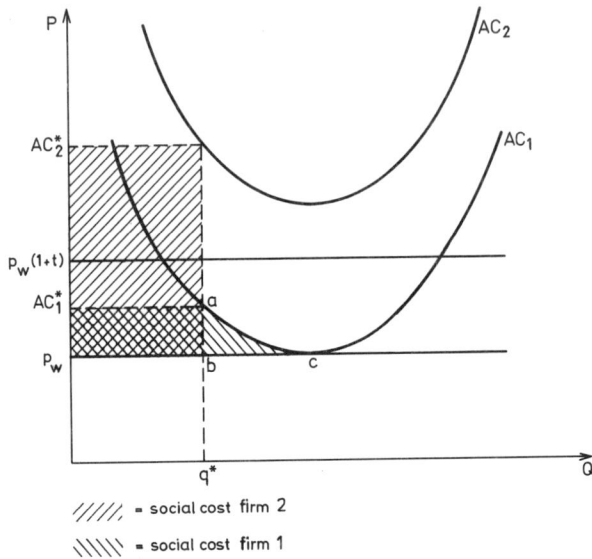

///// = social cost firm 2
\\\\\ = social cost firm 1

profit of q^* $(p_w(1+t) - AC_1^*)$. The social cost of such an institution is very large by the standards of an equivalent per unit output production subsidy of the most efficient firm: all of firm 2's output could be purchased at world market price p_w; the extra social cost of production is q^* $(AC_2^* - p_w)$, which can be decomposed into the absolute subsidy amount plus the firm's output times the difference between domestic and world prices. In addition, this institution is forcing firm 1 to impose a loss on society, namely the extra cost incurred by operating above minimum average cost $(q^* (AC_1^* - p_w))$ plus the extra output and cost reduction foregone (surface abc). Lost consumer surplus attributable to the NTB's in steel should be added as a minor footnote to this social loss.

208. The German steel industry is generally thought to be efficient at domestic prices, and perhaps at world prices [World Bank, 1987], but one German company is not. It is the only one to have received the type of cost transfers analyzed here. It produced 10.3 million tons of rolled steel during the period 1981-1985. The firm received DM3.4 billion in subsidies, or about DM330 per ton [Herdmann, Weiss, 1985]. Had the company ceased production, and had its quotas been transferred to other German firms, so that they could expand output and move down the

average cost curve, this would have saved a total of DM5.7 billion. This would have been sufficient to bribe the company's workers not to work to the tune of DM250 thousand, instead of the DM45 thousand which the laid off workers actually received. The situation in the other European countries is more pronounced still. Six firms, producing 55 million tons of steel in 1981, which received most of the subsidies, received DM46 billion in the five year period to 1985. Had they ceased production, other companies could have produced the steel at a total cost of DM50 billion less. This adds up to a social loss of DM105 billion for the five year period, and ignores consumer surplus, which is dwarfed by these figures in any case.

209. Does it pay (socially) for the government of the low cost producer to subsidize its steel industry? First of all, it does not pay the government of the low cost producers to subsidize the one firm which has high cost by international standards at all. Secondly, there is no point in subsidizing national producers which have minimum average costs above world market prices. In a contestable market without quotas, it does not matter who produces. The only rationale for a subsidy is a political one – keep your own producers afloat until the other, higher cost producers, have cut capacity or gone out of business, or at least use the threat potential to keep down domestic prices below what they otherwise might be. It always pays the low cost producer's government to fight for a higher quota, and if minimum average cost is truly at or below world market prices, to press for liberalization. This has in fact been the strategy of the German government, in accord with the producer's interest organization. The quota system was dismantled from July 1988, but the issue of subsidies is by no means cleared up yet [The Economist, 1988, p. 58]. If this episode is repeated either in steel or in other industries high costs will be incurred through the obverse of Horstmann and Markusen's "inefficient entry", namely insufficient exist. This episode also illustrates well how sensitive strategic trade policy results are to entry and exit conditions, which must lie behind firm's choices of strategies. It is not enough to observe a concentrated industry and infer from that observation that government intervention would lead to gains from trade.

210. While West Germany shows a distinct pattern of change in total effective assistance to industries, it is difficult to map out many implications of that pattern. It seems reasonably certain that the change in assistance impeded externally-induced structural change, as could be shown for the important case of trade with Japan. If one accepts the evolution of the trade structure with Japan as a proxy for the corresponding trade structure of the rapidly-growing economies, then one can infer that the change in protection was generally designed to ward off externally-induced structural change. This observation is consistent with the change in protection favoring physical capital intensive industries and medium-skill intensive industries. At the micro-level, the change in protection inhibited the exit of firms, and so contributed to higher costs. While rationalization investment was observable in industries which received more assistance, this kind of investment is wasted if too many firms remain in the market. Thus, this picture of recent changes in effective protection in West Germany seems to be neither consistent with the aims of industrial policies nor with the necessary adjustment to the international division of labor.

VII. Liberalizing German Trade Policy - General Equilibrium Simulations

211. The previous chapters have discussed various aspects of trade and industrial policy and have sought to summarize their economic impact in part by measures such as the implicit rate of nominal protection and the effective rate of protection including effective subsidization. The explanation for their structure was then investigated through the political economy approach. The objective of the present chapter is to extend the analysis by considering the overall effects of the trade and industrial policy regime. This is done by considering the benefits of a full liberalization, the costs or effects of the present system being the reverse.

1. The General Equilibrium Approach

212. The need for a general equilibrium approach when one is considering the costs of the present trading system can be illustrated by briefly reconsidering the theory of effective protection. As normally derived, the system interactions are taken into account by the input-output technology. However, both balance-of-payments equilibrium and full employment are assumed. The former effect was discussed by Corden [1971] under the heading of "net effective protection". This involves calculating the equilibrium exchange rate, something which can be neglected when one is dealing with a relatively insignificant commodity but which involves general equilibrium calculations when this is not the case. The latter effect is essentially covered by the concept of "true protection" developed by Clements and Sjaastad [1984]. In its simplest form, it involves the transmission of protection across sectors via the reaction of wages to developments in the consumer price index. The labor market and the demand system is thereby taken into account, once again necessitating a general equilibrium approach.

213. An additional factor increasingly stressed is the interaction of the public finance system with trade and industrial policy measures. In the single "small" sector approach to protection, the consequences for gov-

ernment finance of tariff revenues or subsidy outlays can be safely ignored. This is clearly not the case for the trade system as a whole, as can be seen by the fact that in 1980, subsidies amounted to some DM102.6 billion or about 5.5 percent of GNP (Chapter II).

214. In order to take account of these complex interactions, the Kiel Institute's applied general equilibrium model of West Germany was utilized (1). Given the problem at hand a model with 13 sectors was specified. The salient features of the government subsidies they enjoy are documented in Table 23. Apart from the agricultural and food processing sectors, seven manufacturing and three service sectors are modeled. In terms of total protection, the "Gang of Four" are thus explicitly represented: agriculture, coal mining, iron and steel, and clothing and textiles. Not only are those sectors with both much and little protection handled, but also a variation in the nature of protection is considered: for example, agriculture relies to a great extent on subsidies, whereas clothing and textiles are protected in ways which do not directly involve budget transfers (through the MFA).

The allocation of subsidies by sector and use, including the CAP production and export subsidies, is shown in Table 23. Not only is the allocation of subsidies across sectors uneven, but the purposes of the subsidies differ. Whereas in agriculture the bulk of the subsidy is production-oriented, in other sectors it relates primarily to investment and capital. This coupling of subsidy disbursements to a specific base such as output or factor use is potentially important for the factor and commodity composition of trade so that four categories of subsidies are explicitly incorporated.

215. The interested reader is referred to Dicke et al. [1988], for a listing of the model equations. Here a thumbnail sketch of the more impor-

---

(1) The model is derived from the Orani work of Dixon et al. [1982] and an earlier version is documented in Gerken and Gross [1985]. Previous applications include studies on steel subsidies [Gerken et al., 1986], subsidy reductions [Gerken et al., 1985], trade liberalization [Kirkpatrick, 1987a] and agricultural protection [Dicke et al., 1988]. It is currently being further refined and extended [Kirkpatrick, 1988].

Table 23 - Allocation of Subsidies by Sector and Use, 1980/81

Sector	I-O Categories	Share of subsidies (percent)	Distribution of subsidies			
			output	inter-mediates	labor	capital
Agriculture, forestry and fishery	1,2	16.7	48.7	7.7	3.0	40.6
Food and beverages	38-40	0.9	50.3	1.6	7.2	40.9
Coal mining	6	5.9	38.0	18.7	21.9	21.4
Iron and steel	16,18,19	0.4	7.4	18.4	12.7	61.5
Aerospace	25	0.8	6.0	42.5	30.3	21.1
Electrical, engineering, data processing	22,26	1.7	27.7	20.3	29.5	22.4
Metal working and mechanical engineering	20,21,23, 24,28	2.5	22.6	13.3	17.6	46.5
Basic commodities	4,5,7-10,12, 13,17,30,32	1.7	12.1	15.7	9.8	62.5
Other consumer goods	11,14,15,27, 29,31,33-35	1.1	34.8	3.8	12.0	49.4
Textiles and clothing	36,37	0.2	36.4	3.9	13.7	46.0
Housing and construction	41,42,51	17.1	12.2	1.2	1.2	85.4
Market services	3,43-50, 52-55	32.8	23.6	15.4	20.6	40.4
Nonmarket services	56-58	18.3	3.4	14.0	33.2	49.4

Source: Calculated from Tables 6 and 14.

tant features of the model is given. The model belongs to the Johansen class of general equilibrium models; it is linear in percentage changes (i.e. behavioral equations have been log-linearized about a 1980 base year). The equation system can be represented by:

$$Az = 0 \qquad \qquad \qquad ...[1]$$

where A is an m·n matrix of coefficients and z is an n·1 vector of variables written as percentage changes. For a solution, n-m variables must be declared as exogenous allowing the model to be partitioned as:

$$A_1 y + A_2 x = 0 \qquad \qquad \qquad ...[2]$$

and solved as:

$$y = -A_1^{-1} A_2 x \qquad \qquad \qquad ...[3]$$

where y is an m·1 vector of endogenous variables and x an (n-m)·1 vector of exogenous variables.

216. The appropriate choice of exogenous variables and of their values depends on the purpose of the simulation; this is discussed more fully below. However, two categorizations are carried through all simulations. Firstly, all trade barriers and subsidies are represented as exogenous ad valorem instruments which are to be eliminated. The problems involved with representing NTB's by tariff equivalents are well known and much the same problems arise with the treatment of subsidies. However, it is probably beyond the capability of any modelling effort to faithfully represent the diversity of instruments which governments and interest groups have invented. Secondly, the choice of exogenous variables is also governed by the time period under consideration. This chapter is concerned with the medium to long run which is defined as the time required for complete intersectoral mobility of capital and labor. Sectoral capital and labor stocks are therefore endogenous, the exogenous factor being either an aggregate factor rental or an aggregate stock.

217. The model's behavioral assumptions are: domestic commodities are produced by three primary factors (aggregate labor, capital and a sector specific factor called "land") in addition to domestic and foreign intermediate inputs. Labor is further disaggregated into a skilled and an unskilled category, the substitutability between the two being represented by a CES function. Substitutability between the primary factors is rep-

resented by a CRESH (1) production function, but between value added and intermediates, fixed coefficients (Leontief technology) are assumed. The differentiation by skills is important given comparative advantage considerations and the observation that unemployment in West Germany (as in other West European countries) is primarily concentrated in un-skilled (or wrongly skilled) groups [Donges et al., 1988]. The medium-skilled groups of Chapter VI are lumped together with high-skilled groups. But despite the model's long-run nature, there is no mobility of labor between skill groups. Given the technical relationships, factor de-mands are derived through the assumption of cost minimization by firms.

218. The international aspect of the model is conditioned by the assump-tion of imperfect substitutability between home and foreign goods in con-sumption, capital formation and intermediate use. Substitution possibil-ities are represented by an Armington CES system. Household budgeting (i.e. the allocation of expenditures across composite goods) is represent-ed by a linear expenditure system (2). German import demands do not affect world prices, but foreign demand for German exports is governed by finite elasticities; in other words, a large country is being modeled. Protection for German exporters afforded by the EEC is not recognized. The balance of trade is derived in the model by summation over exports and imports, and equality or a predetermined surplus is enforced in the model solution by price changes or exchange rate adjustments. The me-chanism behind Corden's net protective rate [Corden, 1971] is thereby explicitly included: Other things equal, protection will lower imports, resulting in an incipient trade surplus. The real exchange rate will appreciate, and choke off exports, both directly and through induced wage increases.

219. The fiscal system incorporates direct and indirect taxes together with subsidies which also include EEC programs. The level of real gov-

---

(1) Constant Ratio Elasticity of Substitution Homothetic; in contrast to the CES function, CRESH does not restrict all elasticities of substi-tution among pairs of factors to equality. For a description, see Dixon et al. [1982].
(2) This implies the absence of goods complementarity.

ernment expenditure on goods and services is exogenous and held constant. The government budget is balanced, the endogenous policy instrument in all reported simulations being the direct tax rate. Direct taxes will therefore decline as an immediate consequence of budget savings arising from a dismantling of subsidies.

220. With a prespecified balanced government budget and balance of trade, savings and investment behavior requires specification. For this purpose, a procedure from the Orani model [Dixon et al., 1982] is adopted: the ratio of real investment to real consumption is held constant. Investment, in turn, is endogenous, both in the aggregate and in intersectoral allocation, being determined by rates of return.

221. With respect to the labor market, the main simulations undertaken also utilize a non-Walrasian closure: a constant after-tax consumer real wage together with given interskill wage relativities are assumed. This implies that the level of employment is solely determined by labor demand so that either the labor supply curve must be infinitely elastic or there exists an unlimited pool of unemployed. The consumer price index is in turn a function of foreign and domestic goods prices. Thus, two intersectoral transmission mechanisms for trade and industrial policy are incorporated. Along the lines of Clements and Sjaastad [1984], an increase in protection will raise consumer prices, increasing nominal wages and thereby taxing other industries. Similarly, increased taxes to support subsidies will call forth compensating wage changes.

222. This closure is chosen as the reference point because

- current announced policy concerns are directed overwhelmingly towards employment,

- the weight of the evidence points to both structural and real wage rigidity (1) and

---

(1) Evidence of rigidity is given by Knoester and van der Windt [1987], Gundlach [1986], and Trapp, Soltwedel [1988]. Causes for rigidity are increasingly sought in the institutional structure of the German labor market: it lies in the middle of the liberal-to-corporatist spectrum. See especially Bruno, Sachs [1985], Calmfors, Driffill [1987], and DeLong, Jonung [1988].

- a politically feasible reform package will probably have to avoid real wage decreases.

That being said, the shadow price of these assumptions are investigated by comparison to a Walrasian closure.

Finally, domestic goods prices are determined through the zero profits condition. Unless otherwise stated, the capital market is assumed to be integrated both nationally and internationally so that the after tax rate of return is fixed by the world market (i.e. exogenous). Rental prices for sector specific factors completely adjust so as to ensure full utilization.

2. Trade Liberalization

223. The general features of the trade regime are apparent from Simulation 1, Table 24. In this simulation, all implicit tariffs and subsidies are removed. For a linear model individual effects are additive, so that simulations for the removal of tariffs and subsidies alone are also reported. The table indicates that the removal of all subsidies and tariffs would increase output by 4.6 percent and employment by more. However, skilled employment increases by 6.8 percent in comparison to a change in low-skilled employment of 5.3 percent. With given wage relativities, the current trade regime actually seems to discriminate against skilled employment. If at the given wage, this increased supply of skilled labor is not forthcoming, then the implied complementarity of labor types would serve to reduce greatly, if not eliminate, the income gains from liberalization. A notable feature of Table 24 is the contrasting factor proportion effects of the tariff and subsidy systems. Whereas the former appears to favor capital and low-skilled employment relatively, the latter seems to favor capital and high-skilled employment relatively.

224. The factor usage implications are of course difficult to analyze under a regime of perfectly elastic supply, which implies a cheapening of labor relative to capital. Therefore, in Simulation 2 a Walrasian closure,

Table 24 - Effect of Trade Liberalization on Sectoral Output and Aggregate Variables (percentage change)

Production sector	Implicit nominal tariff	Simulation					
		1: complete wage flexibility			2: Walrasian liberalization	3: relative wage flexibility	4: fixed real exchange rate
		tariff	+ subsidy	= full			
1 Agriculture	54.0	-16.2	-24.5	-40.7	-43.1	-43.5	-44.7
2 Food processing	26.7	-8.4	-16.5	-24.9	-27.5	-27.9	-27.7
3 Coal mining	44.2	-17.5	-28.0	-45.5	-51.5	-49.9	-58.4
4 Iron and steel	20.0	5.5	-1.4	4.1	-2.7	0.5	-20.9
5 Basic commodities	4.7	12.8	-0.9	11.9	7.0	7.6	-2.9
6 Aerospace	6.5	15.1	-41.4	-26.3	-33.3	-33.1	-48.2
7 Electrical engineering	5.6	25.0	4.2	29.2	21.8	24.0	2.2
8 Mechanical engineering	6.5	15.1	0.4	15.5	10.1	11.7	0.0
9 Clothing and textiles	28.5	-46.1	6.1	-40.0	-44.7	-41.0	-55.6
10 Other consumer goods	7.4	3.9	1.0	4.9	0.8	1.2	-4.4
11 Construction and housing	0.0	2.8	2.8	5.6	0.4	1.5	13.3
12 Market services	0.0	4.9	-2.8	2.1	-3.2	-2.4	1.5
13 Nonmarket services	0.0	0.3	-0.1	0.2	-0.4	-0.2	0.4
GDP		3.7	0.9	4.6	0.0(a)	1.2	0.4
Real exchange rate(b)		-8.5	3.5	-5.0	-5.2	-4.5	0.0*
Aggregate imports		23.2	2.5	25.7	23.1	23.9	40.0(c)
Aggregate capital		1.8	-1.9	-0.1	0.0*	-4.6	0.8
Net rate of return		0.0*	0.0*	0.0*	-11.5	0.0*	0.0*
Employment - low-skilled		3.1	2.2	5.3	0.0*	8.0	-0.5
- high-skilled		5.2	1.6	6.8	0.0*	0.0*	0.9
Consumer real wage (before tax)							
- low-skilled		2.4^+	-10.3^+	-7.9^+	-6.0	-13.8	-5.9^+
- high-skilled		2.4^+	-10.3	-7.9^+	-4.6	-4.4	-5.9^+
Consumer real wage (after tax)							
- low-skilled		0.0*	0.0*	0.0*	-0.9	-7.4	0.0*
- high-skilled		0.0*	0.0*	0.0*	0.6	2.1	0.0*

(a) In this model, GDP is calculated as the initial income share of each factor times each factor supply. Where factor supplies do not change, as in the Walrasian simulation, GDP does not change. This result is an artifact of the models linearity and obviously has no welfare implications. - (b) Nominal exchange rate divided by consumer price index. - (c) Exports grow by 7.3 percent. The balance of trade consequently deteriorates by DM112 billion in 1980 prices. In this base year the balance of trade was in fact in surplus by DM10 billion. - * exogenously fixed. - + ratio exogenously fixed at unity. - Simulation 1 - Exogenously set at zero change are real after-tax consumer wages, after-tax rate of return on capital and real government expenditures. All tariffs and subsidies are reduced to zero. For the simulation "tariff", only ad valorem tariff rates are eliminated with subsidies remaining. The simulation "subsidy" eliminates subsidies but keeps tariffs. In all three simulations the consumer price index is endogenous, the numeraire being the exchange rate. Simulation 2 - As for Simulation 1 with the exception that the aggregate capital, skilled employment, and unskilled employment are exogenous and set at zero change. Consequently the own factor prices, held constant in Simulation 1, are now endogenous. Simulation 3 - As for Simulation 1 but now the two labor quantities are set exogenously, the two associated wages being endogenous. Simulation 4 - As for Simulation 1 but the consumer price index is set exogenously at zero change. Consequently the balance of trade, exogenously set at zero in the other simulations, is now endogenous.

Source: Own calculations.

in which the aggregate capital and employment stocks are held constant, is reported. Liberalization in this case reduces the returns to capital and low-skilled labor, and raises the returns to high-skilled labor, supporting the impression gained from Simulation 1.

225. Simulation 2 also clearly illustrates the sectoral consequences of the trade regime. Under liberalization, the capital *and* unskilled labor intensive sectors, agriculture, food processing, coal mining and clothing and textiles all sharply contract, expansion being concentrated in basic commodities, electrical and mechanical engineering. In Simulation 1 these latter sectors expand more strongly because the relative price of skilled emplyoment actually falls. A similar effect for unskilled labor reduces the contraction in other sectors and leads to an expansion in the iron and steel and market services sectors. However, the sensitivity elasticities are quite high. Also apparent from Simulations 1 and 2 is the transmission mechanism. Thus the trade expansion effects of liberalization induce a real exchange rate depreciation of around 5 percent. In contrast, a pure subsidy leads to an appreciation.

226. As to be expected, the trade regime has a rather substantial impact on the commodity composition of trade. Table 25 indicates substantial decreases in the net exports of agriculture, coal mining, iron and steel and clothing and textiles. The gainers are basic commodities and the two engineering sectors, in other words those normally regarded as best reflecting West Germany's comparative advantage. Interestingly, market services also strengthens its net export position under both Simulations 1 and 2 even though under the latter simulation market service output decreases. That trade and subsidy policy may inadvertently tax the classic export industries is clearly illustrated by these two simulations.

227. If Simulation 1 represents an infeasible solution due to the implied expansion of skilled employment, then Simulation 2 represents a non-optimal solution due to the presence of unemployment. Simulation 3 therefore reports an external liberalization which is accompanied by an internal liberalization of the labor market to make possible an 8 percent expansion of employment of unskilled labor. Such a combined attack on the problem of unemployment (and growth), justified by labor market rigidities, has been forcefully put forward by Giersch [1986]. Thus, at the same time as reducing unskilled employment through trade liberalization, one also seeks to expand its use in unprotected sectors.

Table 25 - Sectoral Development of Exports and Imports (percentage change)

Production sector	1980 share of		Simulation 1(a)		Simulation 2		Simulation 3		Simulation 4	
	imports	exports	imports	exports	imports	exports	imports	exports	imports	exports
1 Agriculture	7.7	0.7	34.2	-48.6	30.7	-46.6	31.7	-48.6	34.4	-58.1
2 Food processing	5.8	4.0	158.2	5.8	151.3	6.8	157.5	5.2	192.2	-3.6
3 Coal mining	0.4	1.0	587.5	-38.6	595.2	-41.4	593.0	-40.6	633.8	-49.9
4 Iron and steel	3.9	6.1	102.4	45.4	103.0	39.2	100.0	43.8	120.8	11.6
5 Basic commodities	39.7	18.9	2.5	29.4	-0.9	27.7	0.3	27.3	8.7	10.8
6 Aerospace	1.0	0.5	15.9	-11.1	15.7	-17.1	15.6	-17.0	20.8	-35.5
7 Electrical engineering	6.9	9.5	4.2	74.2	4.0	65.0	2.7	68.6	19.8	21.4
8 Mechanical engineering	10.6	32.0	-4.5	41.2	-3.3	36.5	-5.2	38.5	20.4	14.4
9 Clothing and textiles	6.9	3.4	92.6	26.5	90.4	25.7	88.3	27.1	121.9	17.1
10 Other consumer goods	7.5	7.0	2.5	14.8	0.7	14.1	3.1	13.6	34.7	4.4
11 Construction and housing	1.6	2.3	-2.1	0.8	-9.1	2.3	-4.4	0.1	9.8	-5.3
12 Market services	8.0	14.3	-1.7	5.5	-7.1	6.2	-4.1	4.0	4.7	-6.5
13 Nonmarket services	0.0	0.0	0.0	0.0	0.0	0.0	0.0	0.0	0.0	0.0

(a) Removal of both subsidies and implicit tariffs.

Source: Own calculations.

228. Relative wages are quite sensitive to the trade regime: the unskilled after-tax wage falls by 7.4 percent, while the skilled wage rises by 2.1 percent (i.e. a relativity change of around 10 percent). The capital stock falls even though aggregate output increases by around 1.2 percent. The interindustry composition of output, however remains similar to that of Simulation 1. An exception, however, is market services which declines, apparently due to the increased cost of skilled labor. Table 25 also shows a similar development in the commodity composition of trade.

229. The reported simulations have utilized the usual assumption of balanced trade. As a consequence, Simulations 1-3 all indicate an important equilibrating role for the real exchange rate. The consequences of this implicit assumption can be investigated in a little more detail. Simulation 4, Table 25, therefore repeats the full liberalization Simulation 1 but with the real exchange rate now held constant. As a consequence, imports rise by 40 percent in comparison to 25.7 percent for Simulation 1. The growth in exports is restricted to 7.3. percent so that a trade deficit of DM112 billion (1980 prices) emerges. The expansion of GNP is now much smaller (0.4 percent as opposed to 4.6 percent). However, of particular interest is the contrasting pattern of factor utilization. Capital and skilled employment both expand by around 1 percent but unskilled employment falls by 0.5 percent.

230. The changing pattern of factor usage is reflected in industry composition. In comparison with Simulation 1, the three service sectors strongly expand, the expansion in the export industries being relatively weak. Production decreases in agriculture, food, coal mining and textiles somewhat more than for Simulation 1, reflecting the absence of the induced depreciation. The structure of the economy (in comparison with Simulation 1) has therefore shifted away from tradeable to nontradeable goods and services. Put another way, the factors which have led to strong surpluses in the German balance of trade (and therefore a depreciation of the real exchange rate) are the very same factors which have led to a relative underdevelopment of services and an expansion in the engineering sectors. One cannot be discussed independently of the other.

3. Sensitivity Analysis

231. Something about the uncertainty associated with general equilibrium exercises must be said. Two issues are important. Firstly, the exogenous changes in tariffs and subsidies for some sectors are quite large, thereby introducing linearization error. Exactly how important this is cannot be determined a priori but Dixon et al. [1984] report simulations in which the errors average around 40 percent. In their particular example, the macro benefits arising from a complete reduction of tariffs in a *single* sector were overstated. The present reductions affect many more sectors so that the errors may to some extent cancel. However, the experience of Dixon et al. shows that the qualitative results remain essentially unchanged. Secondly, general equilibrium simulations are functions of the chosen parameters. How to interpret results will therefore depend both on the sensitivity of the endogenous variables to a parameter and the uncertainty with respect to the chosen value of the parameter itself (1). In order to give some feel for the relationship between qualitatitve and quantitative results, Table 26 reports the sensitivity elasticity of endogenous variables (the sectoral size changes as well as the macro-aggregates) with respect to two types of parameters: the elasticity of substitution between home and foreign goods in consumption, intermediate use, and investment (39 parameters altogether) and the elasticity of export price with respect to export volume (the inverse of the price elasticity of demand for exprots, 13 parameters altogether). The result are only somewhat sensitive to other parameters; these two categories are especially important.

232. In order to assess sensitivity, the elasticities in Table 26 are considered. An example is useful. The elasticity of GDP with respect to changes in *all* parameters governing goods substitution in the case of full liberalization is -0.62. This would imply that a 100 percent increase in all these parameters would decrease the change in GDP by 62 percent or from 4.6 percent to 1.84 percent. By contrast, the elasticity for GDP in the case of a pure subsidy liberalization is -1.74 so that the GDP

---

(1) For a fuller discussion see Kirkpatrick [1988].

Table 26 - Sensitivity Elasticity of Main Results with Respect to Selected
Parameters (1)

Production sector	Substitution domestic/foreign goods				Export demand elasticity			
	simulation 1			simu-lation 2	simulation 1			simu-lation 2
	tariff	subsidy	full		tariff	subsidy	full	
1 Agriculture	1.25	0.71	0.92	0.78	-0.28	-0.16	-0.21	-0.09
2 Food processing	1.53	0.69	0.98	0.73	-0.55	-0.15	-0.29	-0.09
3 Coal mining	1.34	0.62	0.90	0.75	-0.32	-0.27	-0.29	-0.15
4 Iron and steel	-1.52	-0.52	-1.85	1.84	0.55	-0.97	1.06	0.44
5 Basic commodities	0.58	0.54	0.59	1.48	0.54	-20.4	0.73	0.33
6 Aerospace	0.53	0.42	0.36	0.30	0.37	-0.37	-0.79	-0.50
7 Electrical engineering	0.38	0.57	0.41	0.69	0.12	-0.34	0.05	-0.20
8 Mechanical engineering	0.29	2.09	0.34	0.77	0.14	-2.23	0.08	-0.33
9 Clothing and textiles	1.06	0.85	1.10	0.89	-0.24	0.25	-0.31	-0.12
10 Other consumer goods	0.34	0.89	0.46	6.69	1.75	1.00	1.59	3.04
11 Construction and housing	-0.48	-0.78	-0.63	0.21	1.20	0.43	0.81	-3.36
12 Market services	-0.13	0.83	-1.38	-0.29	0.87	-0.59	2.79	0.09
13 Nonmarket services	-0.37	1.68	-1.77	0.09	1.11	-0.96	2.52	0.16
GDP	-0.35	-1.74	-0.62	-	1.02	1.27	1.07	-
Real exchange rate	0.20	-0.10	0.42	0.53	0.44	-0.10	0.83	0.59
Aggregate imports	0.26	0.41	0.27	0.37	-0.52	-0.21	-0.49	-0.56
Aggregate capital	-1.14	1.38	48.38	-	1.86	-0.69	-48.17	-
Net rate of return	-	-	-	0.18	-	-	-	0.23
Employment - low skill	-0.72	-0.57	-0.66	-	1.30	0.51	0.98	-
- high skill	-0,07	-0,76	-0,24	-	0.76	0.68	0.74	-
Wages - low skill	0.38	0.05	0.21	0.36	0.88	0.09	0.46	0.35
- high skill	0.38	0.05	0.21	0.22	0.88	0.09	0.46	0.42

(1) The sensitivity elasticity is defined as $\partial y/y/\partial \theta/\theta = S_i$ where y are the endogenous variables and θ are specific parameter.

Source: Kirkpatrick [1988].

change of 0.9 percent is totally eliminated by a 100 percent change in
the parameter. Similar sensitivity elasticities also hold for the export
demand elasticity.

233. With respect to goods substitution, the elasticities used are by con-
ventional econometric standards high, so that if anything, income gains
are understated. Also, the export price demand elasticities are high,
which again means that bias with respect to income and employment effects is towards understatement. One can conclude that full liberalization
or pure tariff elimination would surely lead to employment and income
gains. However, for subsidy elimination alone the output effect is less
robust; the primary effect seems to be on factor intensities. Although
the sensitivity elasticity of the capital stock with respect to substitution

and export demand elasticities is quite high, the signs differ between the tariff and subsidy removal experiments. Qualitative judgements about each component of the protective system taken by itself would then be robust. The factor returns implication also appears quite robust.

4. Conclusions

234. The most important result to emerge from this analysis is that trade and subsidy policy do matter both for the level of employment and output and for the pattern of factor use and trade. This may seem rather trite so it should be stressed that many studies do in fact find only very small gains to trade liberalization [see, for example, some of the studies in Srinivasan and Whalley, 1986]. The reason for this difference must be sought in several areas.

235. Firstly, whereas many studies examine only the effects of tariffs, here total assistance to the business sector was analyzed. Whereas the former is usually quite low, the latter, reflecting a range of NTB's, is quite high. Moreover, most studies either fail to take account of subsidies, or when they do, utilize rather low official figures. As noted in Chapter II, the present data show subsidies much higher than those officially reported. On these two grounds alone one would expect higher gains from liberalization than is usual.

236. Secondly, there are important differences in model structure. Perhaps of most importance is, however, the model closure. Whereas most studies seek to model a pure efficiency gain through Walrasian closures (i.e. all markets including labor clear and the balance of trade is zero) the present model allows to presumed rigidities. The choice of model structure is not merely based on theoretical considerations but reflects the judgement that the labor market in West Germany is characterized by rigidity in both the level and structure of wages. Within this framework, one must judge the effects of trade and industrial policy (here understood as subsidy and taxation expenditures). In this respect, the gains

from liberalization (or the costs of the present trade regime) were shown to depend crucially on the supply of skilled labor. To be effective, external liberalization must be accompanied by labor market liberalization which either makes relative wages flexible or promotes the supply of skilled labor. Seen from the political economy of protection perspective, the trade regime is an important flanking measure to particular labor market institutions.

237. If the trade regime has resulted in significant overall losses then it has clearly also resulted in important gains for particular groups. Thus both tariffs and subsidies have had substantial effects on both the sectoral composition of production and trade and with, it returns to sector specific factors. Even where liberalization does not result in great overall gains, the intersectoral shift is clearly significant although numerically imprecise.

238. Not only is sectoral output affected but also the factor content, although here there seem to be important differences between the effects of tariffs and subsidies. At the cost of reduced overall levels of employment, the tariff system appeared to protect capital and unskilled labor relatively, whereas the subsidy system was strongly oriented towards capital, and to a lesser extent skilled labor. Indeed, the subsidy system was shown to have significantly increased the overall capital intensity of production.

239. Finally, the influence of variation in the real exchange on the sectoral composition of employment, output and trade was investigated. Rather unsurprisingly, the very factors which have led to large surpluses in the balance of trade would also have led to a smaller service or nontradeable sector and larger engineering and basic commodity sectors. However, the trade regime as such has not caused this development since it was shown that these classic German export industries have in fact been taxed and therefore restricted.

VIII. Summary and Conclusions

240. The systematization and quantification of trade policy measures taken by itself has already produced pronounced results. While tariffs on the bulk of manufacturing trade have declined through the efforts of the Tokyo Round, where protection and assistance have gone up or remained high, there has been a vengeance in the process. A small, distinctive group of industries has been the main beneficiary of protection:

- agriculture and food processing,

- coal mining,

- the steel industry,

- shipbuilding, and

- textiles and clothing.

These are old, declining industries based on ubiquitous technologies. New industries which have been exceptionally promoted are

- electronic data processing, and

- the aerospace industry.

But assistance to the first industry is high only by the standards of manufacturing as a whole and assistance to the second industry, while remaining high, has declined.

241. As far as subsidies are concerned, they certainly have increased over the last decade and a half. However, industrially broad based subsidy programs, which were only somewhat distortionary through an influence on factor allocation, were displaced by more sector-specific programs. Moreover, the targeted industries consisted of most of the industries already listed. Nothing dramatic happened to subsidization in any other traded goods industry. Quite the contrary, the one high-tech industry which received much in the way of subsidization declined in the degree of public assistance received. Aside from these sector specific programs, however, the diverse ways in which subsidy programs are in-

stitutionalized strongly suggest that there is no centrally-promulgated industrial policy with a coherent set of aims.

242. What have been the consequences of these trade and industrial policies? Are there any patterns in interindustrial patterns to be detected in support policy? For one thing, they have been unsurprisingly effective in what is their underlying aim - to redirect trade flows. The empirical evidence is quite convincing on this score, even for trade flows so notoriously difficult to predict as bilateral ones. Otherwise, very few systematic things can be said about the pattern or the consequences of trade and industrial policy. One is that declining industries have been supported most; another is that policy has not prevented decline. If the protection granted was to lower (social) adjustment cost, alternative policies would have been more successful and less costly. More tellingly, aid to industries increased most that use relatively intensively workers with medium skill levels - crafts persons. The low skilled are not protected and the high skilled are not promoted, but traditional skills in traditional industries were aided most.

Most importantly, on average across industries, trade and industrial policy has promoted "inefficient entry" or "insufficient exit". Average firm size increased least in those industries gaining most from policy. In addition, labor productivity of small firms increased least in those industries where industrial assistance increased most. This is evidence for protection creating high cost producers, inducing them to move "up the average cost curve", but going up backwards.

One specific market where this occurs with a vengeance is the steel industry. An institutionalized system in the EC of granting subsidies to cover firms' losses while imposing production quotas on firms to prevent the losses from getting out of hand has enabled high cost producers to stay in the market. In such a situation, social cost on the production side is greater than the amount of the subsidy. Therefore, the government should not subsidize its high cost producers, of which West Germany has but one.

243. Given the important, perhaps unintended, but above all few discernible features of the interindustrial pattern of industry assistance, the question arises as to what can explain the pattern. Political economy approaches to explaining changes in trade and industrial policy work particularly well for West Germany. Interest groups are in place, even institutionalized, and are able to alter the protective structure in their favor if they are large, or if they have access to government in the form of their own ministries. Moreover, protection has increased most in those industries which have been able to subject themselves to policy automata, where a change in support need not be negotiated and renegotiated year after year through the bureaucratic and political processes. Political economy explanations for changes in the protection structure work better for West Germany than for countries with more pluralist sets of interest groups, because the free rider problem in organizing the groups in the first place has been overcome - a century ago.

244. Nonetheless, interest group interaction with government alone does not explain enough about changes in protection to be entirely convincing. Taking into account national governments' interactions with each other improves the explanation significantly. Governments override the interest groups when it is opportune for them to do so, and it is opportune particularly when the larger issues of foreign policy, but even the more mundane issues of economic policy, are at stake. While this is difficult to show statistically, it can be easily shown historically. Major changes in West Germany's tariff levels and structures have almost always been associated with important foreign policy issues. In this, the founding of the "Zollverein" was no different than the founding of the EC. It is also consistent with Bismarck's moves towards - and away from - free trade, to say nothing of Hitler's move towards autarky. Finally, the emergence of post-World War II Germany's tariff schedule can be understood in no other way, since it was thrashed out between domestic interest groups and foreign governments.

245. The effects of liberalization crucially depend on labor market conditions. Given flexible real wages, the income effects of complete liberalization (though not necessarily partial liberalization) were great, whereas under fixed real wages they were smaller. There is reason to believe

that in West Germany it is the real wage which is the subject and object of negotiation by large established groups, that is to say more or less exogenous with respect to labor market conditions. This book could not investigate labor market conditions, but different assumptions about the labor market were simulated. As expected, the change in income and employment in response to complete liberalization is greatest when wages are completely flexible. This result is obtained if budgetary savings of cutting subsidies are passed on to employers; net wages do not fall.

246. While these results are believed to be firm, some major lacunae in research remain which need to be closed before more confident assessments of the effects of trade policy can be tabled. The most important one is a better integration of new political economy with new industrial policy considerations. It would be important to find out whether recognition that rents can be redistributed internationally through industrial policy leads to activity on the part of firms and organized groups to capture those rents. More concretely, a better assessment of the effects of trade policy - positive or negative - urgently requires more systematic information across firms or industries. One or two case studies are insufficient to establish the efficiency of policy. Moreover, as the case of the steel industry in this study has shown, assumptions on ease of entry into an industry crucially determine policy results. As the steel industry shows, appearances may be deceptive. Therefore, entry conditions must be explicitly addressed, because they surely affect firms' strategies which in turn determine the effects of policy intervention. On the political economy side, a better understanding of the conditions under which governments override interest groups is required. While some effort has gone into studying how members of legislatures will vote on particular issues, or even what stances political parties take at election time, it is probably fair to say, that the supply side of protection is understood less well than the demand side. Lastly, it is probably also fair to say that there exists a tendency for theory to outstrip fact. More attention needs to be given to generating systematic facts. Such tasks will have to be undertaken repeatedly, because the facts collected are crucially codetermined by the theoretical spectacles through which one views the world. Put more positively, as theory gets more refined, so do the facts needed to validate or contradict that theory.

247. Whatever policy conclusions one would or would not draw because of these caveats, perhaps one will bear up and endure: policies actually undertaken have been singularly ineffective when outcomes are compared to announced intentions or even any reasonable interpretation of what intentions could be. This applies to promotion of employment in particular. If the analysis in this study is correct the reason for that outcome is that policies are eventually captured by interest groups. If this is recognized, and policies have to be undertaken at all to help individuals, then the policies should not preserve the interest groups behind the policies. They should aim at the eventual extinction of the groups. The obvious answer to structure preserving policies is direct income transfers, even if these cannot be uniform for everybody. Yes, such a policy will induce lobbying for additional transfers. But this activity is unlikely to be as effective as the lobbying of groups tied to particular places and technologies. The recipients of direct income transfers are likely to live eventually in diverse places and to hold diverse interests. The important thing is to avoid the resource waste of the trade policies; the resources to finance transfer payments would become readily available from trade liberalization, in West Germany albeit predicated upon a concurrent internal liberalization.

Because the supply of protection is relatively poorly understood, these policy conclusions may be beside the point. But some expectation that the domestic and international dynamics of industry support schemes may eventually self-destruct is justified. Firstly, nowhere has protection succeeded in protecting. As employment declines in an industry, so will its power. Secondly, protection has become costly in the visible, budgetary sense. This bodes good, because such measures have more direct information value than do nonbudget measures for politicians and for the general public. Thirdly, interest groups are sometimes inept in the sense that only subgroups benefit much from policy.

248. An important example with international ramifications is agriculture. The workings of EC farm policy have led to what may be the beginning of the dissolution of the solidarity of the farm bloc. The many small, marginal farmers have received no economic rents from farm policy as implemented. They are forming countervailing lobbies. At the same time,

the small farmers understand they would be better off under a system of income, rather than price, supports. It is fortuitous that pressure from the United States to liberalize international trade in agricultural products comes at the same time. It would be particularly helpful for the United States to maintain a hard negotiating line on agriculture, but offering concessions in manufacturing, of course. This, together with pressure from somewhat less protectionist countries in the EC could result in the farm problem being solved more economically in West Germany. Then, within the EC, West Germany could defend its free trade interests and free trade ideology far more effectively and far more credibly, shifting the balance in the Community and the world as a whole towards freer trade.

249. The overall evaluation of trade policy in West Germany is that it

- does not lead to policy pronounced outcomes;

- has many unintended, costly consequences;

- has been - on average - ineffective in promoting or retarding structural change in output and employment;

- probably by design effectively distorts trade flows.

One might object that the reason for this outcome is the poor design of policies. Be that as it may, policies do not follow technocratic blueprints, but they follow the vagaries of the domestic and international political process. Indeed, in pluralist societies, it could not be otherwise. While free trade has been objected to in specific cases and for particular reasons, the alternative general rule - follow industrial policies - can be expected to perform a lot worse, if the evidence for this one country carries any weight.

152

Bibliography

A. Articles and Monographs

ABRAMOVITZ, Moses, "Catching Up, Forging Ahead, and Falling Behind". The Journal of Economic History, Vol. 46, 1986, pp. 386-406.

ADLUNG, Konrad, Hermann GÖTZINGER, Konrad LAMMERS, Instrumente einer patentialorientierten Regionalpolitik. Institut für Kommunalwissenschaften der Konrad Adenauer Stiftung, St. Augustin 1979.

ANDERSON, Kym, Robert E. BALDWIN, The Political Market for Protection in Industrial Countries: Empirical Evidence. World Bank Staff Working Papers, 492, Washington 1981.

ANDERSON, Tyers, Restrictions in World Food Markets: A Quantitative Assessment. Background paper for the World Development Report, World Bank. Washington 1986.

ANJARIA, Shailendra, N. KIRMANI, A.B. PETERSEN, Trade Policy Issues and Developments. IMF Occasional Papers, 38, Washington 1985.

BALASSA, Bela, "Trade Liberalization and 'Revealed' Comparative Advantage". The Manchester School of Economic and Social Studies, Vol. 33, 1965, pp. 99-123.

--, "Tariff Reductions and Trade in Manufactures among Industrial Countries". The American Economic Review, Vol. 56, 1966, pp. 466-473.

--, Trade Liberalization among Industrial Countries: Objectives and Alternatives. New York 1967.

--, The Structure of Protection in Developing Countries. Baltimore 1971.

-- (Ed.), European Economic Integration. Amsterdam 1975.

--, "Japan's Trade Policies". In: Herbert GIERSCH (Ed.), Free Trade in the World Economy: Towards an Opening of Markets. Symposium 1986. Tübingen 1987, pp. 111-170.

--, Constantine MICHALOPOULOS, Liberalizing World Trade. The World Bank, Washington 1985.

BALDWIN, John R., Paul K. GORECKI, "The Determinants of Small Plant Market Share in Canadian Manufacturing Industries in the 1970s". The Review of Economics and Statistics, Vol. 67, 1985, pp. 156-161.

BALDWIN, Robert E., "The Political Economy of Protectionism". In: Jagdish BHAGWATI (Ed.), Import Competition and Response. Chicago 1982, pp. 263-286.

BALDWIN, Robert E. [1985a], "Trade Policies in Developed Countries". In: Ronald W. JONES, Peter B. KENEN (Eds.), The Handbook of International Economics, Vol. I. Amsterdam 1985, pp. 571-619.

-- [1985b], The Political Economy of U.S. Import Policy. Cambridge, Mass., 1985.

BARKIN, Kenneth D., The Controversy over German Industrialization 1890-1902. Chicago 1970.

BAUMOL, William J., "Productivity Growth, Convergency, and Welfare: What the Long-Run Data Show". The American Economic Review, Vol. 76, 1985, pp. 1072-1085.

--, John C. PANZAR, Robert D. WILLIG, Contestable Markets and the Theory of Industry Structure. New York 1982.

BHAGWATI, Jagdish N., "Directly Unproductive Profit-Seeking (DUP) Activities". Journal of Political Economy, Vol. 90, 1982, pp. 988-1002.

--, Richard A. BRECHER, Thirukodikaval N. SRINIVASAN, "DUP Activities and Economic Theory". In: David C. COLANDER (Ed.), Neoclassical Political Economy. Cambridge, Mass., 1984.

BLAICH, Fritz, Staat und Verbände in Deutschland zwischen 1871 und 1945. Wiesbaden 1979.

--, "Protektionismus und unternehmerische Wirtschaft". Zeitschrift für Unternehmensgeschichte, Supplement 37, 1985, pp. 8-55.

BÖHME, Helmut, Deutschlands Weg zur Großmacht - Studien zum Verhältnis von Wirtschaft und Staat während der Reichsgründungszeit 1848-1881. Cologne 1966.

BONDI, Gerhard, Deutschlands Außenhandel 1815-1870. Berlin 1958.

BORCHARDT, Knut, "Protektionismus im historischen Rückblick". In: Armin GUTOWSKI (Ed.), Der neue Protektionismus. Hamburg 1984, pp. 17-47.

von BORRIES, Bodo, Deutschlands Außenhandel 1836-1856. Stuttgart 1970.

BRANDER, James, Barbara J. SPENCER, "International R&D Rivalry and Industrial Strategy". The Review of Economic Studies, Vol. 50, 1983, pp. 707-722.

--, --, "Export Subsidies and International Market Share Rivalry". Journal of International Economics, Vol. 18, 1985, pp. 83-100.

BRECKLING, Jens, Sally THORPE, "Effects of EC Agricultural Policies: A General Equilibrium Approach". Bureau of Agricultural Economics, Canberra 1987.

154

BROCK, William A., Stephen P. MAGEE, "The Economics of Special Interest Politics: The Case of the Tariff". The American Economic Review, Vol. 68, 1978, pp. 246-250.

BRONCKERS, Marco C.E.J., "A Legal Analysis of Protectionist Measures Affecting Japanese Imports into the European Community". In: Jacques H.J. BOURGEOIS et al., Protectionism and the European Community. Deventer 1983, pp. 53-98.

BROWN, Ernest, Henry PHELPS, Margaret H. BROWNE, A Century of Pay. The Course of Pay and Production in France, Germany, Sweden, the United Kingdom, and the United States of America, 1860-1960. London 1968.

BRUNO, Michael, Jeffrey D. SACHS, Economics of Worldwide Stagflation. Oxford 1985.

BUCHHEIM, Christoph, "Deutschland auf dem Weltmarkt am Ende des 19. Jahrhunderts". Vierteljahresschrift für Sozial- und Wirtschaftsgeschichte, Vol. 71, 1984, pp. 199-216.

BURKETT, Tony, "The Federal Republic of Germany". In: Stanley HENIG (Ed.), Political Parties in the European Community. London 1979, pp.....

CALMFORS, Lars, John DRIFFILL, "Centralization of Wage Bargaining and Macroeconomic Performance". Economic Policy, Vol. 3, 1988, pp.13-61.

CASSING, James H., Arye HILLMAN, "Shifting Comparative Advantage and Senescent Industry". The American Economic Review, Vol. 76, 1986, pp. 516-523.

CAVES, Richard, "Economic Models of Political Choice: Canada's Tariff Structure". The Canadian Journal of Economics, Vol. 9, 1972, pp. 278-300.

CHEH, John H., "United States Concessions in the Kennedy Round and Short-Run Labor Adjustment Costs". Journal of International Economics, Vol. 4, 1974, pp. 323-346.

CLEMENTS, Kenneth, Larry SJAASTAD, How Protection Taxes Exporters. Thames Essays, 39, London 1984.

CLINE, William R., The Future of World Trade in Textiles. Washington 1987.

CORDEN, W. Max, "The Structure of a Tariff System and the Effective Protective Rate". Journal of Political Economy, Vol. 64, 1966, pp. 221-37.

--, The Theory of Protection. Oxford 1971.

CRANDALL, Robert W., The U.S. Steel Industry in Recurrent Crisis-Policy Options in a Competitive World. Washington 1981.

DAWSON, William H., Protection in Germany. London 1904.

DAVENPORT, Michael, "The Economic Impact of the EEC". In: Andrea BOLTHO (Ed.), The European Economy - Growth and Crisis. 1980.

DEARDORFF, Alan V., "Testing Trade Theories and Predicting Trade Flows". In: Ronald W. JONES, Peter B. KENEN (Eds.), Handbook of International Economics, Vol. 1. Amsterdam 1984, pp. 467-517.

--, Major Recent Developments in International Trade Theory. Research Seminar in International Economics, Seminar Discussion Papers, 150, University of Michigan 1985.

--, --, "The Effects of the Tokyo Round on the Structure of Protection". In: Robert E. BALDWIN, Anne O. KRUEGER (Eds.), The Structure and Evolution of Recent US Trade Policy. Chicago 1984, pp. 361-388.

--, --, Methods of Measurement of Non-Tariff Barriers. UNCTAD/ST/MD/-28, Geneva 1985.

DeLONG, J. Bradford, Lars JONUNG, Hysteresis, the Corridor, and the Political Economy of Unemployment, 1955-1986. NBER Working Papers, 1988, forthcoming.

DICKE, Hugo, Die Wirkungen strukturpolitischer Maßnahmen in der Ernährungsindustrie. Kieler Studien, 144, Tübingen 1977.

--, Adrian BOTHE, Hans BÖHME, Ernst-Jürgen HORN, Harmen LEHMENT, Eckhard KANTHACK, Henning SICHELSCHMIDT, Joachim ZIETZ, Die EG-Politik auf dem Prüfstand. Kieler Studien, 209, Tübingen 1987.

--, Juergen B. DONGES, Egbert GERKEN, Grant KIRKPATRICK, "The Economic Effects of Agricultural Policy in West Germany". Weltwirtschaftliches Archiv, Vol. 124, 1988, pp. 301-321.

DIXON, Peter B., Brian R. PARMENTER, John SUTTON, David P. VINCENT, ORANI, A Multisectoral Model of the Australian Economy. Amsterdam 1982.

DIXON, Peter B., P.R. PARMENTER, J. SUTTON, D.P. VINCENT, ORANI, "Extending the ORANI Model of the Australian Economy". In: Herbert SCARF, John B. SHOVEN (Eds.), Applied General Equilibrium Analysis. Cambridge, Mass., 1984.

DONGES, Juergen B., Gerhard FELS, Axel D. NEU, Protektion und Branchenstruktur der westdeutschen Wirtschaft. Kieler Studien, 123, Tübingen 1973.

DOUGLASS, C. North, Structure and Change in Economic History. New York 1981.

DOWNS, Anthony, An Economic Theory of Democracy. Cambridge, Mass., 1957.

DUMKE, Rolf H., The Political Economy of German Economic Unification: Tariffs, Trade and Politics of the Zollverein Era. University of Wisconsin Dissertation, Madison 1977.

ERDMANN, Manfred, Die verfassungspolitische Funktion der Wirtschaftsverbände in Deutschland 1815-1971. Berlin 1968.

ECHTERHOF-SEVERITT, "Forschung und Entwicklung in der Wirtschaft". Supplement to Wirtschaft and Wissenschaft, Stifterverband für die deutsche Wissenschaft. Essen, various issues.

ERHARD, Ludwig, Deutschlands Rückkehr zum Weltmarkt. Düsseldorf 1954.

ESCHENBURG, Theodor, Herrschaft der Verbände? Stuttgart 1955.

ETHIER, Wilfried, "The Theory of Effective Protection in General Equilibrium: Effective-Rate Analogues of Nominal Rates". The Canadian Journal of Economics, Vol. 10, 1977, pp. 233-245.

FELD, Werner J., West Germany and the European Community - Changing Interests and Competing Policy Objectives. New York 1981.

FELS, Gerhard, "The Choice of Industry Mix in the Division of Labour between Developed and Developing Countries". Weltwirtschaftliches Archiv, Vol. 108, 1972, pp. 71-121.

--, Axel D. NEU, Reform der Kohlepolitik als Beitrag zur Sicherung der Energieversorgung. Institut für Weltwirtschaft, Discussion Papers, 72, September 1980.

FIELEKE, Norman S., "The Tariff Structure for Manufacturing Industries in the United States: A Test of Some Traditional Explanations". Columbia Journal of World Business, Vol. 11, 1976, pp. 98-104.

FINDLAY, Ronald, Stanislaw WELLISZ, "Toward a Model of Endogenous Rent-Seeking". In: David C. COLANDER (Ed.), Neo-Classical Political Economy. Cambridge, Mass., 1984, pp. 89-100.

FINGER, J. Michael, H. Keith HALL, Douglas R. NELSON, "The Political Economy of Administered Protection". The American Economic Review, Vol. 72, 1983, pp. 452-466.

FISCHER, Wolfram, Die Wirtschaftspolitik Deutschlands 1918-1945. Lüneburg 1961.

--, "Staatsverwaltung und Interessenverbände im Deutschen Reich 1871-1914". In: Carl BÖHRET, Dieter GROSSER (Eds.), Interdependenzen von Politik und Wirtschaft. Berlin 1967, pp. 431-456.

--, Wirtschaft und Gesellschaft im Zeitalter der Industrialisierung - Aufsätze-Studien-Vorträge. Göttingen 1972.

FITZMAURICE, John, "European Community Decision Making: The National Dimension". In: Juliet LODGE (Ed.), Institutions and Policies of the European Community. London 1983.

FRANZ, Wolfgang, Klaus KÖNIG, "The Nature and Causes of Unemployment in the Federal Republic of Germany since the 1970's". Economica, Vol. 53, 1986, pp. 219-244.

FREMDLING, Rainer, Technologischer Wandel und internationaler Handel im 18. und 19. Jahrhundert. Die Eisenindustrien in Großbritannien, Belgien, Frankreich und Deutschland. Berlin 1986.

--, Die Zoll- und Handelspolitik Großbritanniens, Frankreich und Deutschlands vom späten 18. Jahrhundert bis zum ersten Weltkrieg. 1987, unpublished manuscript.

GERKEN, Egbert, Martin GROSS, A Structural Policy Model for the Federal Republic of Germany. Institut für Weltwirtschaft, Kiel Working Papers, 240, October 1985.

--, Karl H. JÜTTEMEIER, Klaus-W. SCHATZ, Klaus-D. SCHMIDT, Mehr Arbeitsplätze durch Subventionsabbau. Institut für Weltwirtschaft, Kiel Discussion Papers, 113/114, October 1985.

--, Martin GROSS, Ulrich LAECHLER, "The Causes and Consequences of Steel Subsidization in Germany". European Economic Review, Vol. 30, 1986, pp. 773-804.

GERSCHENKRON, Alexander, Bread and Democracy in Germany. Berkeley 1943.

GIERSCH, Herbert, Internal and External Liberalization for Faster Growth. Institut für Weltwirtschaft, Kiel Working Papers, 275, November 1986.

GIMBEL, John, The American Occupation of Germany. Stanford 1968.

GINSBURG, Roy H., "The European Community and the Unites States". In: Juliet Lodge (Ed.), Institutions and Policies of the European Community. London 1983.

GLISMANN, Hans-H., Frank D. WEISS, On the Political Economy of Protection in Germany. World Bank Staff Working Papers, 427. Washington, October 1980.

GÖBEL, Heike, Lohnzurückhaltung und gewerkschaftliche Vernunft - Die Politische Ökonomie des Arbeitsmarktes in der Bundesrepublik der 60er Jahre. Kiel Working Papers, 333, September 1988.

GOLDSTEIN, Morris, Mohsin S. KHAN, "Income and Price Effects in Foreign Trade". In: Peter B. KENEN, Ronals W. JONES (Eds.), Handbook of International Economics. Amsterdam 1984.

GOUREVITCH, Peter A., "International Trade, Domestic Coalitions, and Liberty: Comparative Responses to the Crisis of 1873-1896". In: Thomas FERGUSON, Joel ROGERS (Eds.), The Political Economy. New York 1984, pp. 279-299.

GRAF, Kurt H., Die zollpolitischen Zielsetzungen im Wandel der Geschichte. Dissertation, St. Gallen, Winterthur 1970.

GROSS, Martin, "Auswirkungen der Protektion im Textilbereich auf Produktion und Beschäftigung in der Bundesrepublik Deutschland". Die Weltwirtschaft, 1984, No. 1, pp. 79-94.

GROSSMAN, Gene M., J.David RICHARDSON, Strategic U.S. Trade Policy: A Survey of Issues and Early Analysis. NBER Working Papers, Cambridge, Mass., 1985.

GRUBEL, Herbert, Peter J. LLOYD, Intra-Industry Trade. London 1975.

GUNDLACH, Erich, "Gibt es genügend Lohndifferenzierung in der Bundesrepublik Deutschland?" Die Weltwirtschaft, 1986, No.1, pp. 74-88.

HAALAND, Jan I., Victor N. NORMAN, "Introduction: Modelling Trade and Trade Policy". The Scandinavian Journal of Economics, Vol. 893, 1987, pp. 217-226.

HABERLAND, Günther, Elf Jahre staatlicher Regelung der Ein- und Ausfuhr. Abhandlungen aus dem Staatswissenschaftlichen Seminar an der Universität Erlangen, H. 3, 1927.

HAMILTON, Carl B., "An Assessment of Voluntary Restraints on Hongkong Exports to Europe and the USA". Economica, Vol. 53, 1986, pp. 339-350.

HARBRECHT, Wolfgang, Die Europäische Gemeinschaft. Stuttgart 1984.

HEITGER, Bernhard, "Corporatism, Technological Gaps and Growth in OECD Countries". Weltwirtschaftsliches Archiv, Vol. 123, 1987, pp. 463-473.

--, Jürgen STEHN, "Protektion in Japan - Interessendruck oder gezielte Industriepolitik?". Die Weltwirtschaft, 1988, No. 1, pp. 123-137.

HELPMAN, Elhanan, Paul R. KRUGMAN, Market Structure and Foreign Trade. Cambridge, Mass., 1985.

HENDERSON, William O., The Zollverein. Cambridge, Mass., 1904.

HERDMANN, Ute, Frank D. WEISS, "Wirkungen von Subventionen und Quoten - Das Beispiel der EG-Stahlindustrie". Die Weltwirtschaft, 1985, No. 1, pp. 101-113.

HIEMENZ, Ulrich, Kurt von RABENAU, Effektive Protektion. Theorie und empirische Berechnungen für die Westdeutsche Industrie. Schriften zur Angewandten Wirtschaftsforschung, 32, Tübingen 1973.

HINDLEY, Brian, "European Community Imports of VCR's from Japan". Journal of World Trade Law, 1986.

HODGES, Michael, "Industrial Policy: A Directorate-General in Search of a Role". In: Helen WALLLACE, William WALLACE, Carole WEBB (Eds.), Policy-Making in the European Community. London 1977.

HORSTMANN, Ignatus, James R. MARKUSEN, "Up the Average Cost Curve; Inefficient Entry and the New Protectionism". Journal of International Economics, Vol. 20. 1986. pp. 225-247.

JERCHOW, Friedrich, Deutschland in der Weltwirtschaft 1944-1947. Alliierte Deutschland- und Reparationspolitik und die Anfänge der westdeutschen Außenwirtschaft. Düsseldorf 1978.

--, "Außenhandel im Widerstreit: Die Bundesrepublik auf dem Weg in das GATT 1949-1951". In: Heinrich WINKLER (Ed.), Politische Weichenstellungen im Nachkriegsdeutschland 1945-1953. Göttingen 1979.

JOHNSON, Harry G., "Technological Change and Comparative Advantage: An Advanced Country's Viewpoint". Journal of World Trade Law, Vol. 9, 1975, pp. 1-14.

JÜTTEMEIER, Karl H., Deutsche Subventionspolitik in Zahlen 1973-1981. Anlagenband zum zweiten Strukturbericht des Instituts für Weltwirtschaft. Kiel 1984.

--, Subsidizing the Federal German Economy - Figures and Facts, 1973-1984. Institut für Weltwirtschaft, Kiel Working Papers, 279, January 1987.

--, Klaus-W. SCHATZ, "West Germany: Managing without a State Investment Company". In: Brian HINDLEY (Ed.), State Investment Companies in Western Europe. London 1983, pp. 227-262.

--, Konrad LAMMERS, Klaus-W. SCHATZ, Enno F. WILLMS, Auswirkungen der öffentlichen Haushalte auf sektorale Investitionsentscheidungen im Industrie- und Dienstleistungsbereich. Forschungsauftrag des Bundesministers für Wirtschaft, Endbericht. Kiel 1977.

KEESING, Donald B., "Labour Skills and International Trade: Evaluating Many Trade Flows with a Single Measuring Device". The Review of Economics and Statistics, Vol. 47, 1965, pp. 287-294.

--, "Labour Skills and the Structure of Trade in Manufactures". In: Peter B. KENEN, Robert LAWRENCE (Eds.), The Open Economy. Essays in International Trade and Finance. New York 1968, pp. 3-18.

KENEN, Peter B., "Nature, Capital and Trade". The Journal of Political Economy, Vol. 73, 1965, pp. 437-460.

KENWOOD, A. G., A. L. LONGHEED, The Growth of the International Economy, 1820-1980. London 1983.

KINDLEBERGER, Charles P., Economic Response. Cambridge, Mass., 1978.

KING, Mervyn A., Don FULLERTON, The Taxation of Income from Capital: A Comparative Study of the U.S., U.K., Sweden and West Germany - Comparisons of Effective Tax Rates. NBER Working Papers, 1073, Cambridge, Mass., 1983.

KIRKPATRICK, Grant, Liberalizing the Trade Regime in Germany - An Applied General Equilibrium Analysis. Paper presented the Econometric Society European Meeting, Copenhagen, August 1987.

KLEPPER, Gernot, Frank D. WEISS, Doris WITTELER, "Protection in Germany: Toward Industrial Selectivity". In: Herert GIERSCH (Ed.), Free Trade in the World Economy: Towards an Opening of Markets. Symposium 1986. Tübingen 1987, pp. 171-191.

KRIEGER, Christiane, Carsten S. THOROE, Wolfgang WESKAMP, Regionales Wirtschaftswachstum und sektoraler Strukturwandel in der Europäischen Gemeinschaft. Kieler Studien, 194, Tübingen 1985.

KRUEGER, Anne O., "The Political Economy of the Rent-Seeking Society". The American Economic Review, Vol. 64, 1974, pp. 291-303.

KRUGMAN, Paul R., "Is Free Trade Passé?". The Journal of Economic Perspectives, Vol. 1, 1983, pp. 131-144.

LAASER, Claus-F., 'Rentseeking' in deutschen Verkehrswesen. Institut für Weltwirtschaft, Kiel Working Papers, 177, June 1983.

LAMBI, Ivo N., Free Trade and Protection in Germany 1868-1879. Wiesbaden 1963.

LAMMERS, Konrad, Subventionen für die Schiffbauindustrie. Institut für Weltwirtschaft, Kiel Working Papers, 211, October 1984.

LAVERGNE, Real, The Political Economy of U.S. Tariffs: An Empirical Analysis. New York 1983.

LEAMER, Edward E., Sources of International Comparative Advantage - Theory and Evidence. Cambridge, Mass., 1984.

LEONTIEF, Wassily, "Domestic Production and Foreign Trade: The American Capital Position Re-Examined". In: Economia Internazionale, Vol. 7, 1954, pp. 9-45.

LIEPMANN, Heinrich, Tariff Levels and the Economic Unity of Europe. An Examination of Tariff Policy, Export Movements and the Economic Integration of Europe, 1913-1931. London 1938.

LIESNER, H.H., "The European Common Market and British Industry". The Economic Journal, Vol. 68, 1958, pp. 302-316.

LONT, Anke, Lars MATHIESEN, Modelling Market Equilibrium: An Application to the World Steel Market. Center for Applied Research, Bergen 1983.

MAGEE, Stephen P., "Endogenous Tariff Theory: A Survey". In: David C. COLANDER (Ed.), Neoclassical Political Economy. Cambridge, Mass., 1984, pp. 41-51.

--, "The Political Economy of US Protection". In: Herbert GIERSCH (Ed.), Free Trade in the World Economy: Towards an Opening of Markets. Symposium 1986. Tübingen 1987, pp. 368-402.

MAIZELS, Alfred, Industrial Growth and World Trade. Cambridge, Mass., 1963.

MARKUSEN, James R., Anthony J. VENABLES, Trade Policy with Increasing Returns and Imperfect Competition: Contradictory Results from Competing Assumptions. CEPR, Discussion Papers, 120, London 1986.

MARSH, John S., Pamela J. SWANNEY, "The Common Agricultural Policy and the Mediterranean Countries". In: Juliet LODGE (Ed.), Institutions and Policies of the European Community. London 1983, pp. 75-97.

MASAYOSHI; Honma, Yiyiro HAYAMI, "Structure of Agricultural Protection in Industrial Countries". Journal of International Economics, Vol. 20, 1988, pp. 115-129.

MATHIESEN, Lars, Tor WERGELAND, Analyse ar verdens stalmarked. Center for Applied Research, Bergen 1986.

MESSERLIN, Patrick, "The Political Economy of Protectionism: The Bureaucratic Case". Weltwirtschaftliches Archiv, Vol. 117, 1981, pp. 469-496.

METCALF, David, "Employment and Industrial Assistance". In: Alexis JACQUEMIN (Ed.), European Industry: Public Policy and Corporate Strategy. Oxford 1984.

MICHELMANN, Hans J., "The Community Decision Making Process". In: Dominik LAOOK, Panayotis SOLDATOS (Eds.), Les Communautés Européennes en Fonctionnement. Brussels 1981. pp. 141-170.

NAUMANN, Friedrich, Neue deutsche Wirtschaftspolitik. Berlin 1906.

NEU, Axel D., Institutions in the West German Coal Industry. Kiel 1986, mimeo.

NISKANEN, William A., Bureaucracy and Representative Government. New York 1971.

NOGUES, Julio J., Andrzej OLECHOWSKI, L. Alan WINTERS, The Extent of Nontariff Barriers to Imports of Industrial Countries. World Bank Staff Working Papers, 789, February 1986.

OHNISHI, Takeo, Zolltarifpolitik Preußens bis zur Gründung des Deutschen Zollvereins. University of Göttingen Dissertation, Göttingen 1978.

OLSON, Mancur, The Logic of Collective Action. Cambridge, Mass., 1965.

--, The Rise and Decline of Nations. New Haven 1982.

PHILIP, Alan B., "Pressure Groups and Policy Making in the European Community". In: Juliet LODGE, Institutions and Policies of the European Community. London 1983.

PINCUS, Jonathan J., "Pressure Groups and the Pattern of Tariffs". Journal of Political Economy, Vol. 83, 1975, pp. 757-778.

POSNER, Michael V., "International Trade and Technological Change". Oxford Economic Papers, Vol. 13, 1961, pp. 323-341.

RIEDEL, James, "Tariff Concessions in the Kennedy Round and the Structure of Protection in West Germany". Journal of International Economics, Vol. 7, 1977, pp. 133-143.

RODEMER, Horst, Die EG-Agrarpolitik. Kieler Studien, 164, Tübingen 1980.

RONINGEN, Vernon, Alexander YEATS, "Nontariff Distortions of International Trade: Some Preliminary Empirical Evidence". Weltwirtschaftliches Archiv, Vol. 112, 1976, pp. 613-625.

RÖPKE, Wilhelm, German Commercial Policy. London 1934.

ROY, E. J., The Determinants of Tariff and Non-Tariff Trade Restrictions in the United States". Journal of Political Economy, Vol. 89, 1981, pp. 105-121.

SAXONHOUSE, Gary, "What is all this about Industrial Targetting in Japan?". The World Economy, Vol. 6, 1983, pp. 253-274.

SCHMALHOLZ, Heinz, Lothar SCHOLZ, Joachim GUERTLER, Innovation in der Industrie. Struktur und Entwicklung der Innovationsaktivitäten 1979-1982. IfO-Institut, Munich 1985.

SCHMIDT, Klaus-D., Hugo DICKE, Juergen B. DONGES, Hans H. GLISMANN, Bernhard HEITGER, Ernst-J. HORN, Karl H. JÜTTEMEIER, Henning KLODT, Dieter KNOLL, Axel D. NEU, Ronald WEICHERT, Im Anpassungsprozeß zurückgeworfen. Die deutsche Wirtschaft vor neuen Herausforderungen. Kieler Studien, 185, Tübingen 1984.

SCHULZ, Gerhard, "Über Entstehung und Formen von Interessengruppen in Deutschland seit Beginn der Industrialisierung". In: Heinz J. VARAIN (Ed.), Interessenverbände in Deutschland. Cologne 1973, pp. 25-54.

SHOUDA, Yasutoyo, "Effective Rates of Protection in Japan". Japan Economic Studies, No. 11, 1982, pp. 68-70.

SOLTWEDEL, Rüdiger, Peter TRAPP, "Labor Market Barriers to More Employment: Causes for an Increase of the Natural Rate? The Case of West Germany". In: Herbert GIERSCH (Ed.), Macro and Micro Policies for More Growth and Employment. Symposium 1987. Tübingen 1988, pp. 181-225.

SPINANGER, Dean, Joachim ZIETZ, "Managing Trade but Mangling the Consumer: Reflections on the EEC's and West Germany's Experience with the Multifiber Arrangement". Aussenwirtschaft, Vol 41, 1986, pp. 511-531.

SRINIVASAN, Thirukodikaval N., John WHALLEY, General Equilibrium Trade Policy Modeling. Cambridge, Mass., 1986.

STAIGNER, Robert W., Alan V. DEARDORFF, Robert M. STERN, "Employment Effects of Japanese and American Protectionism". In: Dominick SALVATORE (Ed.), The New Protectionist Threat to World Welfare. Amsterdam 1987.

STERN, Robert M., "Testing Trade Theories". In: Peter B. KENEN (Ed.), International Trade and Finance - Frontiers for Research. Cambridge, Mass., 1975, pp. 3-49.

STOECKEL, Andy, Intersectoral Effects of the CAP: Growth, Trade and Unemployment. Bureau of Agricultural Economics, Occasional Papers, 95, Canberra 1985.

SWANN, Dennis, The Economics of the Common Market. Harmondsworth 1984.

TARR, David G., Morris E. MORKRE, Aggregate Costs to the United States of Tariffs and Quotas on Imports. Bureau of Economics Staff, Report to the Federal Trade Commission. Washington 1984.

TREUE, Wilhelm, "Eine preußische 'technologische' Reise in die besetzten Gebiete im Jahre 1814". Vierteljahrschrift für Sozial- und Wirtschaftsgeschichte, Vol. 28, pp. 15-40.

TULLOCK, Gordon, "The Welfare Costs of Tariffs and Theft". Western Economic Journal, Vol. 5, 1967, pp. 224-232.

TYERS, Rodney, Kym ANDERSON, Restrictions in World Food Markets: A Quantitative Assessment. Background Paper for the World Development Report for the World Bank. Washington 1986.

ULLMANN, Hans-P., Der Bund der Industriellen. Organisation, Einfluß und Politik klein- und mittelbetrieblicher Industrieller im Deutschen Kaiserreich 1895-1914. Göttingen 1976.

VENABLES, Anthony J., International Trade, Trade and Industrial Policy and Imperfect Competition: A Survey. CEPR, Discussion Papers, 79, London 1985.

164

--, Alasdair SMITH, "Trade and Industrial Policy under Imperfect Competition". Economic Policy, Vol. 3, 1986. pp. 622-660.

VERNON, Raymond, "International Investment and International Trade in the Product Cycle". Quarterly Journal of Economics, Vol. 80, 1966. pp. 190-207.

--, "The Product Cycle Hypothesis in a New International Environment". Oxford Bulletin of Economics and Statistics, Vol. 41, 1979, pp....

WAEHRER, Helen, "Inter-Industry Skill Differences, Labour Earnings and United States Foreign Trade". In: Peter B. KENEN, Robert LAWRENCE (Eds.), The Open Economy, Essays in International Trade and Finance. New York 1968.

WAELBROECK, Jean, "The 'SPELC' - A Tale of Post-War Western Europe". The World Economy, Vol. 6, 1983. pp. 409-420.

--, "Comment on 'Rent-Seeking and Trade Policy: An Industry Approach'". In: Bela BALASSA, Herbert GIERSCH (Eds.), Economic Incentives. London 1986.

--, "The Logic of EC Commercial and Industrial Policy-Making". In: Alexis JACQUEMIN, European Industry: Public Policy and Corporate Strategy. Oxford 1987.

WALLACE, Helen, "National Bulls in the Community China Shop: The Role of National Government in Community Policy-Making". In: Helen WALLLACE, William WALLACE, Carole WEBB (Eds.), Policy-Making in the European Community. London 1977.

WALLICH, Henry C., Mainspring of the German Revival. New Haven 1955.

WEBB, Steven B., "Tariff Protection for the Iron Industry, Cotton Textiles and Agriculture in Germany, 1879-1914". Jahrbücher für Nationalökonomie und Statistik, Vol. 192, 1977, pp. 336-357.

WEISS, Frank D., The Structure of International Competitiveness in the Federal Republic of Germany. An appraisal. World Bank Staff Working Papers, 571, Washington 1983.

--, "Importrestriktionen der Bundesrepublik Deutschland". Die Weltwirtschaft, 1985, No. 1, pp. 88-100.

WERNER, Horst, Dorit WILLMS, Zollstruktur und Effektivzölle nach der Tokyo-Runde, Die Auswirkungen der Tokio-Runde auf die Tarifeskalation und die Effektivzölle der Bundesrepublik Deutschland und der EG. Cologne 1984.

WHALLEY, John H., "Discriminatory Features of Domestic Factor Tax Systems in a Goods Mobile - Factors Immobile Trade Model: A General Equilibrium Approach". Journal of Political Economy, Vol. 88, 1980, pp. 1177-1202

WIENHOLT, Helmut, Juristische Instrumente des Protektionismus. Beiträge zum internationalen Wirtschaftsrecht und Atomenergierecht, 6, Göttingen 1984.

WITTELER, Doris [1986a], Quantifizierung nichttarifärer Handelshemmnisse. Theoretische Grundlagen und empirische Analyse für die Sektoren Textilien und Bekleidung der Bundesrepublik Deutschland. Schriften zur Textilwirtschaft, Vol. 38. Frankfurt 1986.

-- [1986b], "Tarifäre und nichttarifäre Handelshemmnisse in der Bundesrepublik Deutschland". Die Weltwirtschaft, 1986, No. 1, pp. 136-155.

WURM, Franz F., Wirtschaft und Gesellschaft in Deutschland 1848-1948. Opladen 1969.

ZIETZ, Joachim, "Der Agrarsektor in den GATT-Verhandlungen". Die Weltwirtschaft, 1987, No. 1, pp. 200-211.

B. Statistical Sources, Official Documents, Government Budgets, and Newspaper Articles

BAUMGART, Egon, Sabine BOEHME, Joachim SCHINTKE, Produktionsvolumen und -potential, Produktionsfaktoren des Bergbaus und des Verarbeitenden Gewerbes in der Bundesrepublik Deutschland. Deutsches Institut für Wirtschaftsforschung, Berlin, various issues.

BUNDESMINISTERIUM FÜR ERNÄHRUNG, LANDWIRTSCHAFT UND FORSTEN, Statistisches Jahrbuch über Ernährung, Landwirtschaft und Forsten der Bundesrepublik Deutschland 1985, Bonn 1986.

BUNDESMINISTERIUM DER FINANZEN (BMF), Deutscher Gebrauchszolltarif 1982. Bonn 1982.

DER BUNDESMINISTER FÜR WIRTSCHAFT, Schiffbaupolitik der Bundesregierung. Bundestagsdrucksache V/3290. Bonn 1968.

BUNDESMINISTERIUM FÜR WIRTSCHAFT (BMWi) [a], Begründung zum Entwurf eines Zolltarifgesetzes. Berlin 1950.

-- [b], "Vergleichende Übersicht der Zollbelastung nach dem geltenden deutschen Zolltarif mit den Zollsätzen anderer Länder". In: BMWi (Ed.), Begründung zum Entwurf eines Zolltarifgesetzes. Berlin 1950, Appendix.

COMMISSION OF THE EUROPEAN COMMUNITIES, Amtsblatt der EG. Brussels, various issues.

DEUTSCHER BUNDESTAG [a], Bericht der Bundesregierung über die Entwicklung der Finanzhilfen und Steuervergünstigungen gemäß § 12 des Gesetzes zur Förderung der Stabilität und des Wachstums der Wirtschaft (StWG) vom 8. Juli 1967, Subventionsbericht. Bonn, various biannual issues.

-- [b], Grundsätze der sektoralen Strukturpolitik. Drucksache V/2469. Bonn 1968.

-- [c], Jahresbericht 1985 der Bundesregierung. Drucksache 10/2817. Bonn 1985.

-- [d], Presse- und Informationszentrum, Zur Sache - Themen parlamentarischer Beratung: Fragen der Subventionspolitik. Bonn 1982.

THE ECONOMIST, 2 July 1988, p. 58, "Unshackled".

FINANCIAL TIMES, 16 December 1985.

FRANKFURTER ALLGEMEINE ZEITUNG (FAZ), 28 February 1987.

GENERAL AGREEMENT ON TARIFFS AND TRADE (GATT), Textiles and Clothing in the World Economy. Background Study prepared by the GATT Secretariat. Geneva, July 1984.

HANDELSBLATT, No. 148, 4 August 1988, "Frührente für Bauern bei Aufgabe des Hofes".

IFO-INSTITUT, Wirtschaftskonjunktur. Munich, September 1980; September 1986.

KAISERLICHES STATISTISCHES AMT, Statistisches Jahrbuch für das deutsche Reich. Berlin, various issues.

KREDITANSTALT FÜR WIEDERAUFBAU, Bericht über das Geschäftsjahr 1980. Frankfurt a.M. 1981.

MINISTER DER FINANZEN, Bundeshaushaltsplan für das Haushaltsjahr. Berlin, various issues.

MINISTER DER FINANZEN, Haushaltsplan des Landes Niedersachsen. Hannover, various issues.

MINISTER DER FINANZEN, Landeshaushaltsplan Schleswig-Holstein für das Haushaltsjahr. Kiel, various issues.

ORGANIZATION FOR ECONOMIC COOPERATION AND DEVELOPMENT (OECD), Transparency for Positive Adjustment. Identifying and Evaluating Government Intervention. Paris 1983.

--, National Policies and Agricultural Trade. Paris 1987.

SENATOR FÜR FINANZEN, Haushaltsplan freie Hansestadt Bremen. Bremen, various issues.

SENATOR FÜR FINANZEN, Haushaltsplan der freien und Hansestadt Hamburg für das Haushaltsjahr. Hamburg, various issues.

STATISTISCHES BUNDESAMT [a], Fachserie 4: Bergbau und Verarbeitendes Gewerbe, Reihe 4.1.1: Beschäftigung, Umsatz und Energieversorgung der Unternehmen und Betriebe im Bergbau und im Verarbeitenden Gewerbe. Stuttgart, various annual issues.

-- [b], Fachserie 4: Bergbau und Verarbeitendes Gewerbe, Reihe 4.1.2: Betriebe, Beschäftigte und Umsatz im Bergbau und im Verarbeitenden Gewerbe nach Beschäftigtengrößenklassen. Stuttgart, various annual issues.

-- [c], Fachserie 4: Produzierendes Gewerbe, Reihe 4.1.3: Regionale Verteilung der Betriebe im Bergbau und im Verarbeitenden Gewerbe. Stuttgart, various quatrennial issues.

-- [d], Fachserie 7: Außenhandel, Reihe 7: Außenhandel nach Ländern und Warengruppen der Industriestatistik. Stuttgart, various issues.

-- [e], Fachserie 16: Löhne und Gehälter, Reihe 2.1: Arbeiterverdienste in der Industrie. Stuttgart, various annual issues.

-- [f], Fachserie 16: Löhne und Gehälter, Reihe 2.2: Angestelltenverdienste in der Industrie. Stuttgart, various annual issues.

-- [g], Fachserie 17: Preise, Reihe 2: Erzeugerpreise. Stuttgart, various annual issues.

-- [h], Fachserie 18: Volkswirtschaftliche Gesamtrechnungen, Reihe 1: Konten und Standardtabellen. Stuttgart, various annual issues.

-- [i], Fachserie 18: Volkswirtschaftliche Gesamtrechnungen, Reihe 2, Input-Output Tabellen. Stuttgart 1980.

-- [j], Statistisches Jahrbuch. Stuttgart, various issues.

STATISTISCHES REICHSAMT, Statistisches Jahrbuch für das deutsche Reich, Berlin, various issues.

THE WORLD BANK, World Development Report. Washington 1987.

ZEITSCHRIFT FÜR ZÖLLE UND VERBRAUCHSSTEUERN, Siegburg, various issues.

Institut für Weltwirtschaft an der Universität Kiel

Symposien- und Konferenzbände

Herausgegeben von Herbert Giersch

J. C. B. Mohr (Paul Siebeck) Tübingen

Kieler Studien

Institut für Weltwirtschaft an der Universität Kiel

Herausgegeben von Herbert Giersch
Schriftleitung: Hubertus Müller-Groeling

208. John Cathie, Hermann Dick, Food Security and Macroeconomic Stabilization: A Case Study of Botswana 1965-1984. 1987. XI, 164 S. Broschiert *DM* 51,—. Leinen *DM* 71,—.

209. Hugo Dicke et al., EG-Politik auf dem Prüfstand. Wirkungen auf Wachstum und Strukturwandel in der Bundesrepublik. 1987. XI, 185 S. Broschiert *DM* 56,—. Leinen *DM* 76,—.

210. Andreas Kotzorek, Private Gerichte als Alternative zur staatlichen Zivilgerichtsbarkeit. Eine ökonomische Analyse. 1987. XI, 145 S. Broschiert *DM* 55,—. Leinen *DM* 75,—.

211. Ulrich Hiemenz, Rolf J. Langhammer et al., The Competitive Strength of European, Japanese and US Suppliers on ASEAN Markets. 1987. IX, 136 S. Broschiert *DM* 50,—. Leinen *DM* 70,—.

212. Ugo Fasano-Filho, Bernhard Fischer, Peter Nunnenkamp, On the Determinants of Brazil's Manufactured Exports: An Empirical Analysis. 1987. X, 127 S. Broschiert *DM* 50,—. Leinen *DM* 70,—.

213. Ronald Weichert, Probleme des Risikokapitalmarktes in der Bundesrepublik. Ursachen, Auswirkungen, Lösungsmöglichkeiten. 1987. XIII, 265 S. Broschiert *DM* 59,—. Leinen *DM* 79,—.

214. Grant Kirkpatrick, Employment, Growth, and Economic Policy: An Econometric Model of Germany. 1987. VII, 221 S. Broschiert *DM* 60,—. Leinen *DM* 80,—.

215. Roland Herrmann, Internationale Agrarmarktabkommen. Analyse ihrer Wirkungen auf den Märkten für Kaffee und Kakao. 1988. XII, 325 S. Broschiert *DM* 85,—. Leinen *DM* 105,—.

216. Juergen B. Donges, Klaus-Dieter Schmidt et al., Mehr Strukturwandel für Wachstum und Beschäftigung. Die deutsche Wirtschaft im Anpassungsstau. 1988. XVIII, 242 S. Broschiert *DM* 49,—. Leinen *DM* 69,—.

217. Frank D. Weiss et al., Trade Policy in West Germany. 1988. VIII, 173 S. Broschiert *DM* 49,—. Leinen *DM* 69,—.

218. Klaus-Dieter Schmidt, Erich Gundlach, Investitionen, Produktivität und Beschäftigung. Eine empirische Analyse für die Bundesrepublik Deutschland. 1988. X, 145 S. Broschiert *DM* 46,—. Leinen *DM* 66,—.

219. Harmen Lehment, Fiskalpolitik in offenen Volkswirtschaften. 1988. XI. 235 S. Broschiert *DM* 65,—. Leinen *DM* 85,—.

220. Henning Klodt et al., Forschungspolitik unter EG-Kontrolle. 1988. X, 141 S. Broschiert *DM* 47,—. Leinen *DM* 67,—.

J.C.B. Mohr (Paul Siebeck) Tübingen

Postfach 2040, D-7400 Tübingen
ISSN 0340 - 6989

Weltwirtschaftliches Archiv
Archiv
Review of World Economics

Zeitschrift des Instituts für Weltwirtschaft Kiel
Journal of the Kiel Institute of World Economics

Herausgegeben von Herbert Giersch
in Zusammenarbeit mit Mitgliedern der Wirtschafts- und Sozialwissen-
schaftlichen Fakultät der Christian-Albrechts-Universität Kiel

Schriftleitung: Hubertus Müller-Groeling

Band 124   **1988**   **Heft 2**

Das »Weltwirtschaftliche Archiv« erscheint vierteljährlich. Das Jahresabonnement kostet DM 130,–,
das einzelne Heft DM 36,–. (The »Weltwirtschaftliches Archiv« appears quarterly. The subscription
price for one year is DM 130.–; the price for a single issue DM 36.–)

J. C. B. Mohr (Paul Siebeck) Tübingen
Postfach 2040, D-7400 Tübingen
ISSN 0043 - 2636